AQA English and English Language

Higher Tier

Teacher's Book

GCSE

Lindsay McNab
Imelda Pilgrim
Marian Slee

Series Editor
Imelda Pilgrim

Nelson Thornes

Text © Imelda Pilgrim, Marian Slee, Lindsay McNab 2010
Original illustrations © Nelson Thornes Ltd 2010

The right of Imelda Pilgrim, Marian Slee and Lindsay McNab to be identified as authors of this work has been asserted by them in accordance with the Copyright, Designs and Patents Act 1988.

All rights reserved. No part of this publication may be reproduced or transmitted in any form or by any means, electronic or mechanical, including photocopy, recording or any information storage and retrieval system, without permission in writing from the publisher or under licence from the Copyright Licensing Agency Limited, of Saffron House, 6–10 Kirby Street, London, EC1N 8TS.

Any person who commits any unauthorised act in relation to this publication may be liable to criminal prosecution and civil claims for damages.

Published in 2010 by:
Nelson Thornes Ltd
Delta Place
27 Bath Road
CHELTENHAM
GL53 7TH
United Kingdom

10 11 12 13 14 / 10 9 8 7 6 5 4 3 2 1

A catalogue record for this book is available from the British Library

ISBN 978 1 4085 0602 8

Cover photograph/illustration: Heather Gunn Photography

Page make-up by Integra

Printed and bound in Croatia by Zrinski

Contents

Introducing the new specs		v
Introducing and using the Nelson Thornes resources		viii
Finding a route through the materials		x
Matching grids		xiv

Section A: Reading — 1

Chapter 1	Finding the answer	9
Chapter 2	Grand designs	13
Chapter 3	Story openings	16
Chapter 4	Judging the evidence	19
Chapter 5	Texts in contexts	23
Chapter 6	A twist in the tale	26
Chapter 7	Analysing argument	29
Chapter 8	The writer's point of view	33
Chapter 9	Alternative interpretations	36
Chapter 10	Making comparisons	39
Chapter 11	Making your reading skills count in the exam	42
Chapter 12	Making your reading skills count in the controlled assessment	46

Section B: Writing — 50

Chapter 13	Getting your message across	57
Chapter 14	Making the right choices	61
Chapter 15	Organising writing	64
Chapter 16	Getting the words right	67
Chapter 17	Making sense of sentences	70
Chapter 18	Getting it together 1: non-fiction writing	73
Chapter 19	Getting it together 2: fiction writing	76
Chapter 20	Meeting the needs of your readers	79
Chapter 21	Different kinds of writing	83
Chapter 22	Making your writing skills count in the exam	86
Chapter 23	Making your writing skills count in the controlled assessment	89

Section C: Speaking and listening — 92

Chapter 24	Building skills in speaking and listening	97
Chapter 25	Presenting	100
Chapter 26	Discussing and listening	103
Chapter 27	Creating and sustaining roles	106
Chapter 28	Making your speaking and listening skills count in the controlled assessment	109

Section D: Spoken language — 112

Chapter 29	Choosing and using language	117
Chapter 30	Multi-modal talk	120
Chapter 31	Making your spoken language study skills count in the controlled assessment	123

English essentials — 126

Introducing the new specs

Introduction

The introduction of a new specification is a worrying time for any teacher and subject department. Initially, everything seems different and it takes time to familiarise yourself with what you need to do in order to ensure your teaching meets the requirements of the specification and your students fulfil their potential. This section of the teacher notes is designed to help you understand the demands of the new specifications; the chapters that follow, when used in conjunction with the relevant Student Book, are intended to help you to teach the specifications effectively.

The choices

The first step is to decide which specification your students will study. There are two options:

GCSE English

Unit 1: Understanding and producing non-fiction texts

External examination (80 marks, 40% in total):

- Section A – Reading (1 hour, 40 marks)
- Section B – Writing (1 hour, 40 marks)

Unit 2: Speaking and listening

Controlled assessment (45 marks, 20% in total):

- Presenting (15 marks)
- Discussing and listening (15 marks)
- Role playing (15 marks)

Unit 3: Understanding and producing creative texts

Controlled assessment (90 marks, 40% in total):

- Part A – Understanding creative texts: literary reading (up to 4 hours, 45 marks). Students can undertake up to three separate tasks with 15 marks awarded for each.
- Part B – Producing creative texts: creative writing (up to 4 hours, 45 marks). Students undertake two separate tasks with 15 marks awarded for each plus a further 15 marks for accuracy.

GCSE English Language

Unit 1: Understanding and producing non-fiction texts

External examination (80 marks, 40% in total):

- Section A – Reading (1 hour, 40 marks)
- Section B – Writing (1 hour, 40 marks)

Unit 2: Speaking and listening

Controlled assessment (45 marks, 20% in total):

- Presenting (15 marks)
- Discussing and listening (15 marks)
- Role playing (15 marks)

Unit 3: Understanding spoken and written texts and writing creatively

Controlled assessment (80 marks, 40% in total):

- Part A – Extended reading (up to 4 hours, 30 marks)
- Part B – Creative writing (up to 4 hours, 30 marks)
- Part C – Spoken language study (up to 3 hours, 20 marks)

As you can see, both specifications are exactly the same with regard to Units 1 and 2. However, they differ considerably in Unit 3:

- GCSE English covers the requirements for reading in the National Curriculum. GCSE English Language does not. Students taking GCSE English Language must also study, and be assessed in, GCSE English Literature.
- GCSE English Language offers the opportunity to study spoken English. This is not a requirement of GCSE English.

How to make a choice

Many centres currently enter all students for both English and English Literature and will wish to continue this practice. In such cases, GCSE English Language is the obvious option. Others may decide that one GCSE qualification is appropriate and choose GCSE English. A third option is to choose GCSE English Language for some students and GCSE English for others. Fundamentally, the choices departments make will very much depend on the students they teach, their needs and the needs of the centre.

Assessment Objectives

The first place to start with any specification is the Assessment Objectives. These underpin the areas for study and provide the focus for the testing and assessment of these areas. There is considerable overlap between the Assessment Objectives for GCSE English and those for GCSE English Language, and some significant differences. The numbering and naming of the different areas is initially confusing when looking at the specifications together. The details below are intended to clarify this.

GCSE English: AO1 Speaking and listening

GCSE English Language: AO1 Speaking and listening

- Speak to communicate clearly and purposefully; structure and sustain talk, adapting it to different situations and audiences; use standard English and a variety of techniques as appropriate.
- Listen and respond to speakers' ideas and perspectives, and how they construct and express meanings.
- Interact with others, shaping meanings through suggestions, comments and questions and drawing ideas together.
- Create and sustain different roles.

GCSE English Language: AO2 Study of spoken language

- Understand variations in spoken language, explaining why language changes in relation to contexts.
- Evaluate the impact of spoken language choices in their own and others' use.

GCSE English: AO2 Reading

GCSE English Language: AO3 Studying written language

- Read and understand texts, selecting material appropriate to purpose, collating from different sources and making comparisons and cross-references as appropriate.
- Develop and sustain interpretations of writers' ideas and perspectives.
- Explain and evaluate how writers use linguistic, grammatical, structural and presentational features to achieve effects and engage and influence the reader.
- Understand texts in their social, cultural and historical contexts. **[GCSE English only]**

GCSE English: AO3 Writing

GCSE English Language: AO4 Writing

- Write [to communicate] clearly, effectively and imaginatively, using and adapting forms and selecting vocabulary appropriate to task and purpose in ways that engage the reader.
- Organise information and ideas into structured and sequenced sentences, paragraphs and whole texts, using a variety of linguistic and structural features to support cohesion and overall coherence.
- Use a range of sentence structures for clarity, purpose and effect, with accurate punctuation and spelling.

The Assessment Objectives are intended for teachers. They define the skills that students need to develop and will be required to demonstrate. Clearly students need to know what these skills are. Most students, however, are unable to readily access the specialist language of the Assessment Objectives, a term such as 'to support cohesion and overall coherence' having little real meaning for them. The Student Books use more accessible language to explain the requisite skills to students and, at various stages, to 'unpick' the Assessment Objectives in detail (see pages 139–140).

Areas of overlap between Language and Literature

A quick look at the AOs for GCSE English Literature reveals the extent to which they overlap with those for its partner subject, GCSE English Language. The areas of overlap are highlighted below:

- **AO1:** Respond to texts critically and imaginatively; select and evaluate relevant textual detail to illustrate and support interpretations.
- **AO2:** Explain how language, structure and form contribute to writers' presentation of ideas, themes and settings.
- **AO3:** Make comparisons and explain links between texts, evaluating writers' different ways of expressing meaning and achieving effects.
- **AO4:** Relate texts to their social, cultural and historical contexts; explain how texts have been influential and significant to self and other readers in different contexts and at different times.

Quality of written communication (QWC). Candidates must:

- Ensure that text is legible and that spelling, punctuation and grammar are accurate so that the meaning is clear.
- Select and use a form and style of writing appropriate to purpose and to complex subject matter.
- Organise information clearly and coherently, using specialist vocabulary when relevant.

This demonstrates the extent to which the skills you are developing in your students for GCSE English Language are directly transferable to GCSE English Literature.

Introducing and using the Nelson Thornes resources

Nelson Thornes and AQA

Nelson Thornes has worked in partnership with AQA to ensure that the Student Book, the Teacher's Book and the accompanying online resources offer you the best support possible for your teaching of the GCSE course. The print and online resources together **unlock blended learning**; this means that the links between the activities in the book and the activities online blend together to maximise students' understanding of a topic and help them to achieve their potential.

All AQA-endorsed resources undergo a thorough quality assurance process to ensure that their contents closely match the AQA specification. You can be confident that the content of materials branded with AQA's 'Exclusively Endorsed' logo have been written, checked and approved by AQA senior examiners, in order to achieve AQA's exclusive endorsement.

Student Book

Reading, writing, and speaking and listening – as all teachers of English know – are not distinct and separate entities: reading enhances writing; speaking and listening enable a better understanding of reading, and so on.

The Student Book has been divided into four sections, with a predominant focus on a given area to demonstrate clear coverage of the Assessment Objectives and for clarity of organisation:

- Reading
- Writing
- Speaking and listening
- Spoken language.

However, all sections contain elements of the other areas: for example, reading chapters are interspersed with writing and speaking and listening activities, developing students' skills not only in understanding texts but in articulating that understanding. This is essential if students are to effectively express their response to reading in an exam or controlled assessment situation.

Each section of the Student Book concludes with exam and/or controlled assessment chapters. These chapters draw together the skills developed throughout the section and show students how to apply them in their assessments.

All Student Book chapters include:

Objectives
In this chapter you will:

A list of student-friendly learning objectives at the start of the chapter that contain targets linked to the requirements of the specification.

Activity

Activities to develop and reinforce the skills focus for the lesson.

Check your learning

A list of points at the end of the chapter that summarise what students have covered.

Some (but not all) chapters feature:

Biography **Background**

Biographies and backgrounds provide students with additional information about a writer or a text.

Key terms

Terms students will find it useful to be able to define and understand. The definitions also appear in the glossary at the end of the Student Book.

Make a note

Useful points for students to keep a note of, for example, planning or revision hints.

Review and reflect

Opportunities for peer and/or self-assessment.

Speaking and listening

Specific activities testing speaking and listening skills.

Stretch yourself

Extension activities to take the work in a chapter further.

Top tip

Guidance from the examiners or moderators on how to avoid common pitfalls and mistakes, and how to achieve the best marks in the exam or controlled assessment.

The texts and activities in the Student Book have been chosen by the writers to appeal to students, but no single textbook or set of teacher notes can account for the wide range of young people encountered in the classroom. It is the combination of a good teacher and a good textbook that makes the latter most effective. You know your students best. Be prepared to use the materials in the Student Book selectively, to introduce your own texts and activities and to add explanation or differentiated criteria. In this way you will best suit the needs of the students who sit in front of you, and maximise the potential of the Student Book.

Teacher's Book

The Student Book provides a structured route for the development of the skills denoted by the Assessment Objectives. The Teacher's Book acts as a guide to the Student Book, drawing your attention to specific points of focus, providing answers to and guidance on the activities, and suggesting alternative approaches and possible extension work. It is not intended to be in any way prescriptive.

Each section of the Teacher's Book follows the order of the Student Book and includes chapter-by-chapter guidance on using the Student Book resources. It is not, however, essential that you follow the order of the chapters, and it is anticipated that teachers will create their own order from which to work through the chapters, moving between the sections to ensure variation in the primary focus on reading, writing, speaking and listening, and spoken language study.

In addition to the chapter-by-chapter coverage, each section also contains at the start:

- an overview of the section and the AOs
- a resources overview listing all the activities in the Student Book, along with the worksheets and interactive resources available online in *kerboodle!*
- a student checklist, which can be used to assess knowledge and understand before, during or after working through a section; it also indicates which chapters of the Student Book might be useful for consolidation of that particular skill
- a range of activities from the Student Book that can be used to assess student progress through the section
- a list of general resources that could be used to develop the teaching and learning from that section.

To enable you to track your coverage of the specifications, and to build in links with the AQA GCSE English Literature specification and Functional English standards, the grids on pages xiv–xvi provide full coverage of where the units of the specification are taught. In addition, some possible routes through the materials are suggested on pages x–xiii.

Online resources

The online resources are available on *kerboodle!*, which can be accessed via the internet at www.kerboodle.com live, anytime, anywhere. If your school or college subscribes to *kerboodle!* you will be provided with your own personal log-in details. Once logged in, you can access your course and locate the required activity.

Throughout the Student Book and Teacher's Book, you will see a *k!* icon whenever there is a relevant interactive activity available in *kerboodle!*. Also within *kerboodle!* you will find chapter-by-chapter guidance on how to use each interactive activity, along with additional worksheets to enhance the material from the Student Book.

Please visit kerboodle.helpserve.com if you would like more information and help on how to use *kerboodle!*.

Finding a route through the materials

The chapters in this course can be used flexibly with students. However, you might find the following notes useful, in conjunction with the matching grids on pages xiv–xvi, to help you decide which chapters will meet particular teaching and learning targets and which will most appeal to your students.

Section A: Reading

The order of the chapters in the Reading section has been carefully planned so that students can follow a route of clear progression through the Assessment Objectives. However, the chapters can be grouped to reinforce particular skills as and when required. Some suggested groupings are given below:

Suggested grouping	Skills reinforced
Chapter 2: Grand designs Chapter 3: Story openings Chapter 4: Judging the evidence	These chapters all focus on analysis and evaluation of linguistic, grammatical, structural and presentation features, and how writers use these to engage and influence their readers. The use of structural features is further developed in Chapter 6: A twist in the tale.
Chapter 5: Texts in contexts Chapter 6: A twist in the tale	These chapters develop the Unit 3 requirement to 'understand texts in their social, cultural and historical context' and focus particularly on literary texts.
Chapter 7: Analysing argument Chapter 8: The writer's point of view Chapter 9: Alternative interpretations	These chapters can be used to develop students' abilities to develop and sustain detailed comments. They also reinforce the importance of interpreting the texts and using evidence to support these interpretations.
Chapter 10: Making comparisons	This chapter looks in particular at the skill of comparing texts.

Section B: Writing

As with Reading, the order of chapters in Writing has been carefully thought through to ensure that students have a clear route through the skills, and opportunities for progress checking.

Suggested grouping	Skills reinforced
Chapter 13: Getting your message across Chapter 15: Organising writing Chapter 17: Making sense of sentences	These chapters provide opportunities for students to practise writing in a range of sentence structures; to punctuate their sentences correctly; and to select sentences appropriate to their form, purpose and audience.
Chapter 14: Making the right choices Chapter 16: Getting the words right Chapter 20: Meeting the needs of your readers	These chapters all focus on adapting forms, vocabulary and linguistic features to suit audience and purpose.
Chapter 18: Getting it together 1: non-fiction writing Chapter 19: Getting it together 2: fiction writing	These chapters could be used as summative chapters in which students draw on their prior learning and skills to organise their ideas and information to write whole texts.

Section C: Speaking and listening

Specific guidance on Speaking and listening is given in Section C, along with how this will be assessed. However, there are opportunities throughout the rest of the Student Book to give students practice in these skills. For example:

Links to other sections	Speaking and listening practice opportunities
Section A: Reading Chapter 3: Story openings	• Group discussion on the techniques writers use in the openings of *The Kite Runner*, *Pride and Prejudice* and *Holes*.
Chapter 6: A twist in the tale	• Group discussion on the context and historical background to 'The Weapon', along with its relevance for current scientific developments.
Chapter 8: The writer's point of view	• The Stretch yourself activity is to role-play an interview with Tennyson about his reasons for writing 'The Charge of the Light Brigade' and the techniques he uses in it.
Section B: Writing Chapter 13: Getting your message across	• Activity 9 about ambiguous meanings of newspaper headlines can be done as a paired discussion.
Section D: Spoken language Chapter 30: Multi-modal talk	• Group discussion in Activity 4 to establish the conventions of texting.

In addition:

- many of the activities can be undertaken as paired work
- the Review and reflect activities can be done in pairs, with students reviewing and assessing each other's work.

Section D: Spoken language

This section of the Student Book provides guidance on Unit 3, Part C of the GCSE English Language specification – the Spoken language study. Chapter 29 provides an introduction to thinking about the contexts of and influences on spoken language, while Chapter 30 focuses on the impact of new technologies on spoken language.

These chapters can be used as the basis for a discrete unit of work or can be linked to the other chapters, for example:

Chapters in other sections	Spoken language links
Section B: Writing Chapter 14: Making the right choices	• The analysis of the language used in text messages could be linked with multi-modal forms.
Section C: Speaking and listening Chapter 25: Presenting	• The segments on Standard English and speeches could be linked with considering how context, purpose and audience can affect spoken language.

Links to the AQA scheme of work

The following chapters can be used as starting points to support the scheme of work for Unit 1 published on the AQA website: http://web.aqa.org.uk/aqa-english-resource-zone

Topic outline	Relevant resources from the Student Book and *kerboodle!*
Approaching non-fiction texts	**Chapter 1: Finding the answer** Students identify key information and details in texts; select appropriate material to answer questions; explain how writers use words to affect their readers. **Chapter 15: Organising writing** Students think about how texts are organised and structured, and how ideas and information are organised into sentences and paragraphs.
Features of non-fiction texts	**Chapter 2: Grand designs** Students investigate how texts are organised and think about the ways that presentational features are used for effect. **Chapter 14: Making the right choices** Students explore how language and form can be adapted to suit purpose and audience, including using emails and letters.
Close reading skills	**Chapter 3: Story openings** Students explore the language techniques used by writers and the effect these have on the reader. **Chapter 7: Analysing argument** Students understand and explain the ideas expressed by writers; they examine how writers use language to influence their readers. **Chapter 16: Getting the words right** Students use a range of vocabulary and think about how they will engage their audience through language choices. **Chapter 17: Making sense of sentences** Students think about how they can match their sentence structures to their audience and purpose, and how they can use sentences to express their ideas, emphasise meaning and create effects.
Comparing texts	**Chapter 10: Making comparisons** Students study two texts, thinking about audience and purpose, use of presentation features and use of language. They study the features of a written comparison and write their own comparison. **Chapter 18: Getting it together 1: non-fiction writing** Students explore ways of planning, organising and structuring their non-fiction writing. **Chapter 21: Different kinds of writing** Students practise writing in a range of genres.
Producing and completing an exam paper	**Chapter 11: Making your reading skills count in the exam** Students learn how reading skills are tested in the exam, study texts and questions in a sample paper and consider how to improve their marks. **Chapter 22: Making your writing skills count in the exam** Students learn how their writing skills are tested in the exam; study questions in a sample paper; plan, write and assess and answer; and review examiner's comments to find out how to achieve the best marks.

Links to the *AQA Anthology*

The skills required for GCSE English Literature Units 1A (Modern texts), 2A (Anthology) and 5 (Exploring poetry) are built into and developed throughout the chapters of the *GCSE English and English Language Higher Tier* Student Book. These are indicated in the matching grids on pages xiv–xvi. However, the following chapters provide specific coverage of the texts from the *AQA Anthology*.

Poetry
- **Chapter 5: Texts in contexts**

  Exploring the language used in 'Quickdraw' by Carol Ann Duffy; analysis of 'Futility' by Wilfred Owen, both with and without contextual information and reflection on what impact understanding the context has.

- **Chapter 8: The writer's point of view**

  Students develop and sustain interpretations about 'The Charge of the Light Brigade' by Alfred, Lord Tennyson, from the cluster on Conflict. They are encouraged to consider the background to the poem to inform their comments, to use evidence from the text and to offer interpretations of the evidence.

- **Chapter 12: Making your reading skills count in the controlled assessment**

  Two poems from the Place cluster are used as the basis of the example question and answer, 'Below the Green Corrie' by Norman MacCaig and 'Storm in the Black Forest' by D.H. Lawrence.

- **Chapter 23: Making your writing skills count in the controlled assessment**

  'London' by William Blake is used as the starting point for a 'Prompts and re-creations' creative task.

Short stories
- **Chapter 19: Getting it together 2: fiction writing**

  Students explore the structure of 'Compass and Torch' by Baines before using this as the starting point for their own creative writing.

Links to the set texts

As for the *AQA Anthology* texts, the skills required for the following GCSE English Literature units are built into and developed throughout the chapters of the *GCSE English and English Language Higher Tier* Student Book:

- **Unit 1:** Exploring modern texts
- **Unit 2:** Poetry across time
- **Unit 3:** The significance of Shakespeare and the English Literary Heritage
- **Unit 4:** Approaching Shakespeare and the English Literary Heritage
- **Unit 5:** Exploring poetry.

These are indicated in the matching grids on pages xiv–xvi. The Student Book and *kerboodle!* also include texts from a wide range of authors from the English Literary Heritage, including Chaucer, Austen, Dickens, Orwell and Dylan Thomas. However, the following chapters provide specific coverage of the set texts from the GCSE English Literature specification.

Chapters	Specific coverage of set texts
Chapter 3: Story openings	Students explore Austen's use of dialogue to reveal character in the opening of *Pride and Prejudice* (Unit 4).
Chapter 15: Organising writing	Students use an extract from *Lord of the Flies* (Unit 1) as an example of how writers link ideas within paragraphs.
Chapter 20: Meeting the needs of your readers	Students analyse an extract from *Great Expectations* (Unit 4) to find out how Dickens builds up a range of details to engage the reader.
Chapter 21: Different types of writing	An extract from *Of Mice and Men* is used to exemplify how texts can be adapted into different genres.

Matching grids

The tables that follow outline how the resources link to the units of each of the specifications (GCSE English, GCSE English Language and GCSE English Literature), as well as the Functional English standards, and can be used when planning a scheme of work.

In addition to this, they indicate for each chapter the text types used and written; the speaking and listening focus; and the spoken language focus as appropriate. This information can be used to plan lessons and target particular student needs.

Section A: Reading — GCSE English: AO2 Reading
GCSE English Language: AO3 Studying written language

Chapter and AO focus	English and English Language units	Literature units	Functional English standards	Text types used
1: Finding the answer • Read and understand texts, selecting material appropriate to purpose.	1A 3A	1–5	R1.1, 1.2, 1.3 R2.1, 2.2, 2.3	• Radio guide • Novel • Textbook • Travel guide • Magazine article
2: Grand designs • Explain how writers use structural and presentational features to achieve effects and engage and influence the reader.	1A 3A	1–5	R1.1, 1.3 R2.3, 2.5	• Poster • Flyer
3: Story openings • Explain how writers use linguistic and grammatical features to achieve effects and engage and influence the reader.	1A 3A	1–5	R1.2, 1.3 R2.3, 2.5	• Extracts from the openings of novels
4: Judging the evidence • Evaluate how writers use linguistic, grammatical, structural and presentational features to engage and influence the reader.	1A 3A	1–5	R1.3 R2.3, 2.5	• Magazine article
5: Texts in contexts • Understand texts in their social, cultural and historical contexts.	3A	1 3/4		• Poetry
6: A twist in the tale • Explain and evaluate how writers use structural features to achieve effects and engage and influence the reader.	3A		R2.5	• Fable • Short story • Webpage • Newspaper article
7: Analysing argument • Read and understand texts, selecting material appropriate to purpose.	1A 3A	1–5	R1.1, 1.2, 1.3 R2.1, 2.2, 2.3	• Magazine articles • Newspaper articles
8: The writer's point of view • Develop interpretations of writers' ideas and perspectives.	1A 3A	1 2/4 and 5	R2.3, 2.4	• Autobiography • Poetry
9: Alternative interpretations • Develop and sustain interpretations of writers' ideas and perspectives.	3A	1 2/4 and 5	R2.3, 2.4	• Newspaper article • Autobiography
10: Making comparisons • Collate from different sources and make comparisons and cross-references as appropriate.	1 3A	2 and 3/5	R2.5	• Charity leaflets

Section B: Writing		GCSE English: AO3 Writing GCSE English Language: AO3 Studying written language		
Chapter and AO focus	English and English Language units	Functional English standards	Text types written	
13: Getting your message across • Write [to communicate] clearly.	1B, 3B	W1.1, 1.4, 1.5 W2.1, 2.5, 2.6	• Using tenses and punctuating sentences and paragraphs correctly • Advice/guidance leaflet for Year 7	
14: Making the right choices • Write [to communicate] clearly, effectively and imaginatively, using and adapting forms appropriate to task and purpose (focus on non-fiction forms).	1B, 3B	W1.3 W2.3	• Text message poem • Letter: expressing opinion	
15: Organising writing • Organise information and ideas into structured and sequenced sentences and paragraphs.	1B, 3B	W1.2 W2.2	• Articles for website or magazine expressing opinion • Descriptive paragraph and opening	
16: Getting the words right • Write [to communicate] clearly, effectively and imaginatively, using and adapting forms and selecting vocabulary appropriate to task and purpose in ways that engage the reader.	1B, 3B	W1.3 W2.3	• Descriptive writing including a range of linguistic features	
17: Making sense of sentences • Use a range of sentence structures for clarity, purpose and effect.	1B, 3B	W1.2, 1.4, 1.5 W2.2, 2.4, 2.5, 2.6	• Articles giving information and advice • Persuasive speech • Descriptive writing	
18: Getting it together 1: non-fiction writing • Organise information and ideas into structured and sequenced sentences, paragraphs and whole texts, using a variety of linguistic and structural features to support cohesion and overall coherence (non-fiction).	1B	W1.2 W2.2, 2.4	• Multiple-sentence paragraphs • Newspaper article to express a point of view	
19: Getting it together 2: fiction writing • Organise information and ideas into structured and sequenced sentences, paragraphs and whole texts, using a variety of linguistic and structural features (fiction).	3B		• Mini-saga • Autobiographical writing • Creative writing with a twist • Poetry	
20: Meeting the needs of your readers • Write [to communicate] clearly, effectively and imaginatively, using and adapting forms and selecting vocabulary appropriate to task and purpose in ways that engage the reader.	1B, 3B	W1.3 W2.3	• Autobiographical writing • Review (positive or negative) • Persuasive article • Descriptive writing	
21: Different kinds of writing • Write [to communicate] clearly, effectively and imaginatively, using and adapting forms and selecting vocabulary appropriate to task and purpose in ways that engage the reader.	1B, 3B	W1.3 W2.3	• Writing for different genres inspired by one photograph • Radio script • Poetry	

Section C: Speaking and listening — GCSE English: AO1 Speaking and listening / GCSE English Language: AO1 Speaking and listening

Chapter and AO focus	English and English Language units	Functional English standards	Speaking and listening focus
24: Building skills in speaking and listening • Speak to communicate clearly and purposefully.	2	SL1.1, SL1.2, SL1.3, SL1.4 SL2.1, SL2.2, SL2.3, SL2.4	• What makes a good speaker/listener • Setting targets for improvement
25: Presenting • Speak to communicate clearly and purposefully; use Standard English and a variety of techniques as appropriate.	2	SL1.2, SL1.4 SL2.2, SL2.4	• Language choice and audience • Using Microsoft PowerPoint • Analysing speeches and presentations • Understanding the level descriptors
26: Discussing and listening • Interact with others.	2	SL1.1, SL1.2, SL1.3 SL2.1, SL2.3, SL2.4	• Identifying listening skills • Asking questions • Expressing views and commenting on others' views • Identifying strengths and weaknesses
27: Creating and sustaining roles • Create and sustain different roles.	2		• Using gestures, vocabulary and tone to create characters • Working in pairs and small groups • Using literary texts as the basis for role play

Section D: Spoken language — GCSE English Language: AO2 Study of spoken language

Chapter and AO focus	English Language unit	Spoken language focus
29: Choosing and using language • Understand variations in spoken language, explaining why language changes in relation to contexts. • Evaluate the impact of spoken language choices in their own and others' use.	3C	• Differences in spoken and written language • Mixed and blended modes: instant messaging, texting
30: Multi-modal talk • Understand variations in spoken language, explaining why language changes in relation to contexts. • Evaluate the impact of spoken language choices in their own and others' uses.	3C	• Spoken language in contexts • Recording speech, transcripts • Adapting spoken language • Public speech

Section A: Reading

Overview

Section A of the Student Book is designed to develop students' skills in reading as defined by the Assessment Objectives for GCSE English (AO2 Reading) and GCSE English Language (AO3 Studying written language) and tested in the exam and the controlled assessments.

GCSE English: AO2 Reading
GCSE English Language: AO3 Studying written language

- Read and understand texts, selecting material appropriate to purpose, collating from different sources and making comparisons and cross-references as appropriate.
- Develop and sustain interpretations of writers' ideas and perspectives.
- Explain and evaluate how writers use linguistic, grammatical, structural and presentational features to achieve effects and engage and influence the reader.
- Understand texts in their social, cultural and historical contexts. **[GCSE English only]**

The chapters provide opportunities for students to draw on and revise the skills they have already acquired in reading, and to develop these further. The learning objectives, founded in the Assessment Objectives but in 'student-friendly' language, are given at the start of each chapter. Throughout each chapter the learning points are clarified and modelled, and followed by activities that are designed to reinforce and extend students' learning.

Students are encouraged to work independently or in pairs or small groups, as appropriate, and are given regular opportunities to assess their personal progress and that of other students, often against fixed criteria. The learning within the chapters is cumulative, building on what has come before, and at the end of several chapters there is a summative activity that challenges students to demonstrate their learning across the whole section.

Each chapter can be used as a discrete stand-alone topic, with activities and tasks specific to the named objectives. The order in which they appear in the Student Book does not have to be followed, though it is worth noting that this order was arrived at after careful consideration of how best to build students' skills in reading.

Assessment

GCSE English	*GCSE English Language*
External examination: Reading non-fiction texts (1 hour)	**External examination:** Reading non-fiction texts (1 hour)
Controlled assessment: Understanding creative texts (up to 4 hours)	**Controlled assessment:** Extended reading (up to 4 hours)

English and English Language Teacher's Book Higher Tier
Section A: Reading

Nelson Thornes resources

Chapter	Student Book activities	kerboodle! resources
1: Finding the answer	1–3: Identifying different types of texts and why you might read them 4: Describing the features of texts 5: Reading for information 6: Identifying presentational features 7: Selecting and recording information 8–9: Identifying implied meaning 10–11: Identifying bias	• Planning activity: Social networking sites • Audio role-play activity: Podcast • Research activity: Obesity • Worksheet 1a: Reasons for reading • Worksheet 1b: Recording information • Worksheet 1c: Identifying bias
2: Grand designs	1–3: Identifying purpose and audience 4–6: Exploring the links between text and images 7: Examining the structure of a text 8: Examining colour choices in a text 9: Identifying presentational features in a text 10–11: Commenting on features 12–16: Further work on purpose and audience Stretch yourself: Writing a commentary on a flyer, describing and commenting on structure and presentation Stretch yourself: Designing own poster to appeal to students	• Analysis activity: Car safety • Planning activity: Analysing an electronic text • Write and assess activity: Comparing non-fiction texts • Worksheet 2a: Choosing words • Worksheet 2b: Purpose and audience
3: Story openings	1: Suggesting ideas for a good opening to a novel 2–3: Analysing the opening of *The Kite Runner* and looking for clues 4: Analysing the language used in the novel opening and suggesting alternatives 5: Identifying ways in which the writer creates mood in the novel opening 6–8: Exploring how writers use speech to reveal character 9: Analysing how writers use characters to present their point of view 10: Finding examples of irony and explaining their use 11–13: Analysing techniques writers use to create tone Speaking and listening: Reviewing all three novel openings 14: Deciding which novel opening has most effect on the reader Stretch yourself: Examining and writing about the techniques used by the writer in a novel opening	• Viewpoints activity: Effective openings to novels • Learning activity: Word choices 1 • Learning activity: Word choices 2 • Analysis activity: Story openings • Worksheet 3a: Selecting words

Section A
Reading

Chapter	Student Book activities	kerboodle! resources
4: Judging the evidence	1: Making notes on how structure, presentational features and language are used in a text 2: Using responses to 1 to establish the purpose and audience of a text 3: Explaining the effect of structure, presentation and language in a text 4–5: Reading and annotating a sample response to an evaluative question 6–7: Writing an evaluative response to a text 8: Self-assessment of the response to Activity 7	• Learning activity: Analysing an online newspaper 1 • Learning activity: Analysing an online newspaper 2 • Planning activity: A comparison of two climate change websites • Planning activity: A comparison of two educational websites • Worksheet 4a: Evaluation 1 • Worksheet 4b: Evaluation 2 • Worksheet 4c: Analysing an example answer
5: Texts in contexts	1: Reading texts from different times (Chaucer and Duffy) and suggesting meanings 2: Identifying dialects and suggesting examples 3: Identifying how and why writers use dialect 4: Highlighting cultural references in a text and the difficulties these might present to a reader 5: Paired discussion of students' own culture; writing a paragraph introducing their culture to a stranger 6–9: Responding to questions about the context of a poem, 'Futility' 10–11: Thinking about the context and historical impact of 'The Soldier' by Rupert Brooke 12: Contrasting the attitudes of the poet in 'Futility' to those in 'The Soldier' Stretch yourself: Writing a poem or short story linked to a current news item	• Viewpoints activity: The social context of a novel • Planning activity: Responding to a pre-20th century text • Analysis activity: Analysing texts from other cultures
6: A twist in the tale	1: Finding out the meaning of 'narrate' 2: Analysing the narrative structure of a fable 3: Deciding on the chronological order of events from a narrative 4–5: Analysing the narrative structure of 'The Weapon' 6: Writing a developed response to a question on the structure of 'The Weapon' 7–8: Making notes on one character from 'The Weapon' Speaking and listening: Group discussion on the context of 'The Weapon' Stretch yourself: Writing a fable for modern times	• Viewpoints activity: Making predictions • Analysis activity: The writer's intention • Planning activity: Examining a character • Worksheet 6a: Get the story straight
7: Analysing argument	1: Sorting the order of key points in an article 2: Identifying facts and the reasons for using them in an article 3: Identifying opinions and the reasons for using them in an article 4: Practising referring to a text when answering a question	• Planning activity: Analysing an argument • Webquest activity: How are teenagers represented in the press? • Analysis activity: Understanding the writer's point of view

English and English Language Teacher's Book Higher Tier
Section A: Reading

Chapter	Student Book activities	kerboodle! resources
	5: Identifying rhetorical questions and explaining their use in a text 6: Explaining why a writer has used emotive language in a text 7: Writing an unbiased title for an article 8: Explaining the intention behind biased phrases and rewriting them to make them more neutral 9–10: Writing a developed response to explain how a writer presents an argument in a text	• Worksheet 7a: Wild thoughts
8: The writer's point of view	1: Developing a personal response to a text 2: Analysing a text to find out more about the writer's opinion 3: Using evidence from the text to interpret meaning 4: Sharing first impressions of 'The Charge of the Light Brigade' 5: Deciding on an interpretation of the poem 6: Using evidence from the poem to interpret the meaning 7: Using an example student answer to identify features of a sustained interpretation 8: Writing a sustained interpretation of 'The Charge of the Light Brigade' 9: Examining the poet's viewpoint in the poem Stretch yourself: Role playing an interview with Tennyson about 'The Charge of the Light Brigade'	• Viewpoints activity: Developing an understanding of a character • Write and assess activity: Facts and opinions • Planning activity: The writer's perspective • Worksheet 8a: Interpreting texts • Worksheet 8b: Sustaining an interpretation 1 • Worksheet 8c: Sustaining an interpretation 2
9: Alternative interpretations	1: Responding to questions to interpret a writer's point of view 2: Paired discussion of quotations from a text to establish alternative interpretations 3: Writing a developed response explaining the writer's point of view and offering alternative interpretations 4: Commenting on the impact the writer's choice of language has on the reader 5: Analysing an example answer and continuing this to explain how the writer uses language to reveal opinions 6: Paired discussion on the techniques a writer uses to express her opinions 7: Writing a developed response that offers alternative interpretations of a text and explores the writer's use of language Stretch yourself: Analysing the writer's views and feelings and use of language in text of the student's choice	• Viewpoints activity: Forming an impression • Analysis activity: Understanding the cultural context of a text • Planning activity: The writer's viewpoint • Worksheet 9a: Interpreting the writer's ideas • Worksheet 9b: Your personal response

4

Section A
Reading

Chapter	Student Book activities	kerboodle! resources
10: Making comparisons	1: Identifying the purpose and audience of two texts and highlighting those common to both 2: Identifying presentational features in the two texts, commenting on their effectiveness and highlighting any features common to both 3: Writing detailed comments on the presentational features of one of the texts 4–5: Identifying and making notes on the use of language features in the two texts 6: Writing a developed comment about the use of language features in the texts 7: Writing a comparison of two texts Stretch yourself: Preparing a revision guide for students on how to write a good comparison	• Analysis activity: Comparing teen magazine websites • Analysis activity: Comparing motorcycle safety websites • Planning activity: Making comparisons • Worksheet 10a: Comparing purpose and audience • Worksheet 10b: Comparing presentational features
11: Making your reading skills count in the exam	1: Making notes on possible answers to sample exam questions 2: Identifying skills students have shown in two sample responses to an example Question 1; offering advice for improvements 3: Identifying ways in which a sample answer to an example Question 2 could be improved 4: Practising writing comments for an example Question 3 5: Identifying why one sample answer would gain more marks than another in response to an example Question 4; writing a response to an example Question 4 and peer-assessing this	• Write and assess activity: The Reading exam 1 • Write and assess activity: The Reading exam 2 • On your marks activity: The Reading exam 3 • Worksheet 11a: Analysing sample answers to Question 1 • Worksheet 11b: Analysing sample answers to Question 4
12: Making your reading skills count in the controlled assessment	1: Annotating a text to show the writer's relationship with nature in response to a 'Themes and ideas'-based task 2: Identifying which is the better of two sample answers in response to a 'Themes and ideas'-based task and why 3: Advising a student on how to improve their sample response	• Write and assess activity: The Reading controlled assessment 1 • Connecting comments activity: The Reading controlled assessment 2 • Planning activity: The Reading controlled assessment 3 • Worksheet 12a: Answering a question on Themes and ideas • Worksheet 12b: Analysing a student's response

5

English and English Language Teacher's Book Higher Tier
Section A: Reading

Student checklist worksheet

Read through the following list of skills that you will be expected to demonstrate in your Reading work for GCSE English or GCSE English Language.

Rate your own skills using the columns as a tick chart and then check out which chapters might be most suited to help you tackle any areas you are not sure about.

Skill	Very confident	Quite confident	Sometimes I can	Often I can't	Which chapters might help?
Read texts and show I understand them					1
Choose relevant and appropriate material to answer questions					1
Explain how writers organise texts					2, 4
Explain how writers use presentational features					2, 4
Explain how writers use linguistic features					3, 4
Explain how writers use grammatical features					3, 4
Relate texts to their cultural, social and historical contexts					5
Identify how writers use narrative in a text					6
Understand and explain the ideas expressed by writers in texts					7, 8
Interpret a writer's point of view and ideas					7, 8
Develop detailed comments about a text					9
Express my own views about a text					9
Recognise that there might be different interpretations of the same text					9
Make comparisons between texts					10

Use your responses to the checklist to set yourself *no more than* three targets to achieve from the Reading section.

1. ....

2. ....

3. ....

Section A
Reading

Checking students' progress

The tasks below are all included in the Student Book and can be used to check student progress in a particular skill.

Chapters	AO focus	Activities from Student Book and learning outcomes
1–4	• Read and understand texts, selecting material appropriate to purpose. • Explain and evaluate how writers use linguistic, grammatical, structural and presentational features to achieve effects and engage and influence the reader.	**Chapter 4, Activity 7** Students: • comment on and evaluate organisation, presentational features, language use in a text • make a judgement as to the effectiveness of the article.
5	• Understand texts in their social, cultural and historical contexts.	**Chapter 5, Activities 10–12** Students: • analyse 'The Soldier' by Rupert Brooke, thinking in particular about the intended audience and the impact it might have had at the time it was written • consider the contrasting message in 'Futility' by Wilfred Owen.
6–9	• Develop and sustain interpretations of writers' ideas and perspectives.	**Chapter 7, Activity 10** Students: • write an explanation of how an argument is presented in a text (Text C on page 44) • focus on how the writer develops their argument and the techniques used to do so. **Chapter 9, Activity 7** Students: • write sustained interpretations of views of the author of Text D (page 56) • provide alternative interpretations • support these with textual detail • give their own opinion.
10	• Collate and make comparisons and cross-references as appropriate.	**Chapter 10, Stretch yourself** Students: • provide advice on making comparisons to other students in the form of a revision guide.

English and English Language Teacher's Book Higher Tier
Section A: Reading

General resources

The resources in the Student Book, Teacher's Book and *kerboodle!* provide a range of learning opportunities for students and give them practice at developing their skills using a wide variety of text types. The resources suggested below can be used to reinforce, develop and extend students' skills and learning further.

Type of resource	Author and title
Further reading	Short stories in the *AQA Anthology*: • Haruki Murakami: 'On Seeing the 100% Perfect Girl One Beautiful April Morning' • Elizabeth Baines: 'Compass and Torch' • Penelope Lively: 'The Darkness Out There' • Helen Dunmore: 'My Polish Teacher's Tie' • Clare Wigfall: 'When the Wasps Drowned' • Leila Aboulela: 'Something Old, Something New' • Ridjal Noor: 'Anil' *A Thousand Splendid Suns* by Khaled Hosseini Additional resources to support social, historical and cultural contexts: • Students could be encouraged to read more around the First World War when studying Chapter 5 – for example, Sassoon, Gurney, Thomas, Rosenberg, Brittain. Extracts from *All Quiet on the Western Front* would also provide further background.
Films/DVDs	• There are plenty of film versions of the texts available – for example, *Of Mice and Men*, *To Kill A Mockingbird*, *Romeo and Juliet*. • *Regeneration* is available on DVD and can be used to support work on the context of the poetry of the First World War in Chapter 5.
Websites	• Reading plenty of newspaper articles provides excellent preparation for the Unit 1A exam. Most newspapers have a website on which it is possible to find recent news stories. Alternatively, www.thebigproject.co.uk/news can be used to access a number of local and national newspapers. • More on the background to the First World War can be found at www.firstworldwar.com • Khaled Hosseini's own website (www.khaledhosseini.com) has an accessible video of him talking about his writing which can be used in conjunction with Chapters 3 and 5.

1 Finding the answer

AO focus

English AO2 Reading and English Language AO3 Studying written language.

- Read and understand texts, selecting material appropriate to purpose.
- Explain how writers use linguistic features to achieve effects and influence the reader.

In this chapter your students will:

- read texts and show their understanding of them
- select appropriate material to answer questions
- explain how writers use words to affect the reader.

Additional resources

Worksheets

1a: Reasons for reading
1b: Recording information
1c: Identifying bias

Getting started

Before starting the chapter you could ask students to jot down five different texts they would use to find out things – that is, texts that supply information. Collate these on the board. They might include:

- telephone directories
- TV schedules
- textbooks
- encyclopaedias
- newspapers
- magazines
- signs
- leaflets
- food packaging labels
- maps.

From the collated list, highlight the texts that can be accessed in electronic as well as paper form.

Working through the chapter

Reasons for reading

The aim of this section is initially to help students realise how much they already know about the visual appearance of texts. Students are at the start of their GCSE course and it is important that, right from the beginning, they realise they are building on what they have already learned in English. They can very easily recognise or make assumptions about the content of a text by its appearance.

Activity 1

Text	Distinguishing features
A: Road sign	found outdoors; shape of sign; drawing of roundabout; colour blue for motorways; motorway symbol; capitals and numbers for names of roads
B: Radio guide	times; columns; size of print
C: Textbook extract	diagram; heading and subheadings; question box
D: Online film booking page	PG, 12A and 15 symbols; titles; tickets, time and information symbols; in rows
E: Novel extract	title; continuous prose set across page; paragraphs

Activity 2

Text	Distinguishing features
A	to find out correct road to take – might read all or part, depending on how well you know your route
B	to find out what's on – might read all or part, depending on what time you have available
C	to learn about a subject – would probably read all of it so as not to miss important information
D	to find information about what films are currently showing – might read all if just looking for anything to watch or part if looking for a particular film
E	for enjoyment – would read all if enjoying it

Activity 3

a Students should aim to record a typical school day's reading (Worksheet 1a). Remind them to include things they might read while travelling, playing computer games and in internet chatrooms, as well as the more obvious things.

b Students need to be made aware of the importance of private reading early in their GCSE course. Reading widely has a direct effect on the development of their skills, not only in reading but also in writing and in speaking and listening. For many able students, wider reading is a key element in achieving the highest grades. It is worth noting that, while some students may read a lot, the content of their reading is not particularly demanding and they need to be set in a new direction. You could encourage students to share titles of fiction and non-fiction books that they have read and enjoyed. Alternatively, or additionally, you could draw up a list of recommended reading and set a challenge for them to read all that is on it by the time they have completed their GCSE course. This may include regular reading of a broadsheet newspaper or a 'high-quality' magazine.

Activity 4 Students can choose any text. They should focus on its distinguishing features in their description, without revealing what it is.

Reading for information

Planning activity: Social networking sites

This section focuses on locating information. You may find it useful to set students an initial time challenge of 3 minutes.

Activity 5

a Brooklyn
b the streets
c JFK and Newark
d an unlimited ride MetroCard
e the 'Off Duty' part of the roof light is lit
f subway stations and the Visitors' Bureau in Columbus Square
g Broadway
h any bridge and tunnel tolls
i to allow time for the bus to reach the right terminal
j there are more crosstown routes

Activity 6 Signposts: subheadings; paragraphs; bold print for keywords.

As an extension activity, or homework, you could ask students to find and copy an information text, such as the one given in the Student Book, and to set their own questions on it. These could then be distributed randomly in the class for further practice on locating information.

Finding the right details

Audio role-play activity: Podcast

Webquest activity: Obesity

While students will have used some skills in scanning in order to complete Activity 5, the details they needed were very clearly signposted. This section focuses on the development of skills in scanning using a text written in continuous prose. You might want to spend a few minutes talking with the students about the value of good scanning skills in research. Increasingly, teachers report that students simply print materials from the internet in response to an information research homework. This is of very little value. They need to learn how to scan the material and select the parts that are relevant to their area of study.

Activity 7 An example of a completed table is provided below. A blank table is supplied on Worksheet 1b.

Date	Time	Place	Eye witnesses	Distinctive features
23 July 2008	7.50am	Close to Soham	Alan Cleve	Inky black Spanned 1.4m rails
23 July 2008	Evening	Near Shrewsbury, Shropshire	Lorraine Fletcher Chloë Fletcher	Taller and longer than German shepherd dog Muscular Jet black Big paws Long curled tail Large cat head Little pointed ears Loud growl
23 July 2008	5.20pm	Road between Easton and Weston, Portland Bill, Dorset	Martin O'Neill (prison officer)	About the size of an Alsatian Tan colour with stripes on back Cat's face and ears with huge eyes Long tapered tail with fur 2–3 inches long

Chapter 1
Finding the answer

Working out the meaning

This section moves students on from location and use of detail for purpose to a focus on how writers try to influence their readers. The ability to detect implications and subtlety of a text is a high-level skill and is a regular feature of subsequent chapters. Students need constant reinforcement of this skill throughout their GCSE course. It is required for perceptive reading of non-fiction and fiction and is directly transferrable to GCSE English Literature studies, where this applies.

Activity 8

1. The inverted commas suggest that someone other than the writer has said these sightings are reliable. This could imply that the writer may not agree and causes the reader to question the reliability of the sightings. Alternatively, the writer may have used inverted commas to emphasise the reliability of these sightings, implying that other sightings are not so reliable.
2. The use of the word 'revealed' suggests that the information has been uncovered or, perhaps, kept secret for some time.
3. This emphasises that the information about the sightings was not given voluntarily. A specific request was made before it was revealed, implying that the authorities wanted to keep it secret.
4. The use of the words 'separate' and 'different', when combined in this way, create the impression that there could be more than one large cat.
5. This detail leads the reader to trust the reports of the sightings. 'Very experienced' rangers would be unlikely to make a mistake.
6. We are not told what the other ranger believed. He or she may not have believed it was a big cat.

Activity 9 Accept any valid response that is supported by reference to the text and demonstrates an awareness of implied meaning. A likely interpretation is that the writer wants the reader to think that these sightings are valid ones and that the reports should be taken seriously.

Identifying bias

This section acts as a development from the previous one and as an introduction to bias. Bias is covered in detail in a subsequent chapter (see Chapter 7). When considering the questions in Activity 10, you may wish to alert students to the relevance of tone. The questions may be answered orally or in writing.

Activity 10 The following are possible answers. They are not prescriptive.

Word/phrase	Implication/why chosen
wasting	suggests there is no point in doing this; chosen to persuade reader to writer's point of view
so-called	used in a sceptical way to undermine the reliability of the sightings and make the reader think the accounts are false
we are told	the tone is cynical and leads the reader to compare what they are 'told' with their own actual experience
expensive resources	the emphasis is on the first word in this phrase: 'expensive'; the writer is drawing attention to the cost of the exercise, presumably to make the reader think it is a waste of money
alleged	this word emphasises the absence of proof in the sightings, again to make the reader doubt their reliability
delivered obediently	this makes the police sound as though they are powerless and simply follow orders, perhaps to make the reader feel angry with them
almighty	this suggests that they are very powerful and rule the police, probably used to turn the reader against the Big Cats group

Activity 11 Students can use their responses from Activity 10 to form the basis of their paragraph.

Stretch yourself

While there is no extension activity in the Student Book, a possible activity is given below. Encourage students to explore in detail the language used by the writer. They should aim to compile a comprehensive list of techniques used by the writer, with supporting examples. It is likely that the brightest students will move beyond areas covered in this chapter to identify sentence structures and particular rhetorical devices, in addition to specific words and phrases.

[*continued overleaf*]

English and English Language Teacher's Book Higher Tier
Section A: Reading

Working in pairs or a small group, read the text below (Worksheet 1c), which is the rest of the letter from the Student Book. Discuss how the writer's bias is shown to the reader through what he says and the way he says it. Make a note of any particular techniques the writer uses.

For every sighting there are, we are told, numerous other unreported ones. Excuse me for asking but, if they are unreported, how do we, or indeed anyone, know of their existence? And yet, for all these sightings, reported or not, and for all the efforts of our brave police force, not a single shred of proof exists to support the fairytale notion that these animals are indeed roaming our countryside. Not one recovered skeleton, not one confirmed paw print, not one killed by traffic and not a single photograph. And this, despite the best efforts of all those desperate to prove the case. Perhaps these creatures have the ability to cloak themselves in invisibility whenever a camera draws near?

Never mind, the believers rant. They are there. We will prove it. And so it continues, much in the vein of the deluge of UFO sightings in the seventies. Creatures like cats – taller, broader, faster, with eyes (let's not forget the eyes) that shine in the dark: yellow eyes, green eyes, brown eyes and no doubt some day soon, gleaming golden eyes. These cats have much in common with those aliens from space.

But it's not the sightings of the overactive imaginations that get to me. Live and let live is my motto. If they want to believe there are dangers in the wood, then let them keep out of it. No, it's not them. But the police and the public resources paid for by our taxes? Now that is a different matter. Never mind. Next time I'm burgled or see a ram raider in action or hear a cry for help in my street, I'll call the police. I'll tell them I've seen a BIG CAT. No doubt they'll be at my door within the minute.

Outcomes

In this chapter your students have:

- identified distinguishing features of texts
- located information in a text
- selected material for a specific purpose
- considered how writers use words to influence the reader.

2 Grand designs

AO focus

English AO2 Reading and English Language AO3 Studying written language.

- Explain how writers use linguistic, structural and presentational features to achieve effects and engage and influence the reader.
- Read and understand texts, selecting material appropriate to purpose.

In this chapter your students will:

- investigate how two texts are organised
- consider the ways presentational features are used for effect.

Additional resources

Worksheets

2a: Choosing words
2b: Purpose and audience

Getting started

In Chapter 1 students gave some consideration to the visual appearance of texts and their ability to recognise what a text was from its appearance without actually reading it. Before starting this chapter you could invite students to look around the classroom and list all the different types of texts they can see, for example:

- posters
- students' work
- timetables
- fire notices.

Ask them to select three distinctly different texts and to identify features of each one's appearance, its intended purpose and its intended audience. Although the terms 'purpose' and 'audience' are defined in the Student Book, most students are aware of the meaning of the terms, though not always of their relevance. The intention here is to establish the clear link between appearance, purpose and audience, and you may wish to discuss the relationship between these in the texts they have selected.

Working through the chapter

Purpose and audience

As suggested above, most students are aware of the terms 'purpose' and 'audience'. They are not, however, always aware that:

- texts often have more than one intended purpose and one intended audience
- structure and presentation are directly linked to purpose and audience
- comments on features of structure and presentation need to demonstrate understanding of purpose and audience.

The poster used here is about knife crime. This is a very relevant but potentially sensitive area for students. In the course of this chapter, you may wish to set aside time for discussion of issues relating to knife crime in which students are allowed to share their experiences within small groups or the class as a whole.

Activity 1 The aim is to get students to think about the potential range of purposes of the poster. In addition, you could ask them to find evidence to support each of these intended purposes before they move on to prioritising them. There is no correct order, though (a) and (e) should feature at the top of the list or close to it.

Activity 2 Students are encouraged to discuss their order with another student, though you may find it more useful to discuss this as a class and to agree a priority order, with clear reasons for it.

Activity 3 This raises issues to do with intended audience. Disagreement is likely to revolve around teenage boys/girls and may well be linked to students' own experience, or lack of experience, of knife crime. It may be worth discussing the extent to which the gender of the central figure, seemingly a boy, influences the reader's perceptions.

Content

The aim of this section is to help students understand that the intended form of a text, in this case a poster, has a direct impact on content. This issue is raised again later in this chapter. Activities 4, 5 and 6 are supported by Worksheet 2a.

Activity 4 Here students are required to consider the wording in direct relation to purpose and audience. They are likely to point out that the writer is inviting them to step into the shoes of the boy in the picture through the directive 'Imagine'. There is a clear emphasis on the direct and personal targeting of the reader through the use of the pronouns 'your' and 'you'. The word 'mate' is used intentionally to suggest a close personal relationship. It would be worth asking students why the word 'mate' was used rather

13

English and English Language Teacher's Book Higher Tier
Section A: Reading

than the word 'friend'. More able students could be encouraged to engage with the clever shifts in tense – the ambiguity in 'this **was** your mate', the immediacy of 'you **know**', and the conditional use of 'would' as opposed to 'will'.

Activity 5 This is an engaging poster and challenges students to consider how we 'read' and interpret images. Students could do this activity on their own, but it might be more constructive if they work in groups and then for you to take their points as part of a class discussion. Ask them to consider things such as background scene, mood and clothing, as well as the sequence of events.

Activity 6 This activity invites students to explore the links between the main text, the images and the Crimestoppers logo and information. Structurally the logo is the last thing the reader sees and it is highlighted through the use of a white background. The word 'anonymously' closely reflects the story of the poster, where nothing is given away, not even the appearance of the witness.

Pictures can often present a useful stimulus for writing and it would be possible to break away from the chapter after Activity 6 and ask students to write a paragraph describing a dangerous street at night or, alternatively, to write a story using the picture as a starting or ending point.

Structure

The first part of this section invites students to consider an alternative way of structuring the detail on the poster. The aim of this is to lead them to a clear understanding that designers consider structure in direct relationship to purpose and audience. As well as the alternative structure provided on this page, you could ask students to suggest other possibilities. A consideration of structure, and the possibilities for alternatives, can also be applied to other areas of reading and writing. It challenges students to think of alternative structures and how they would be more or less effective. Hopefully, it also leads them to the use of more imaginative structures in their own writing.

Activity 7 Responses to questions (a) to (f) can be written, but they would be better used as a basis for discussion. The intention is to get students to read the images closely and to draw inferences based on what they see. Discussion could take place in pairs, small groups or as a class, with the answers being collated on the board. If the answers are spoken, it would be useful to then ask students to write a paragraph in response to the question: Why do you think the designer of this poster structured the detail in this particular way?

Presentational features

Analysis activity: Car safety

Early in their GCSE course, students are generally able to identify features of presentation, describe them and make simple comments on them. This section invites them to demonstrate what they know about such features and provides you with an opportunity to assess the quality of their comments. The ability to develop and sustain intelligent comment is essential if students are to achieve high grades when they take their GCSE exam.

Activity 8 You may wish to give additional prompts, such as: What things/ideas/feelings do you associate with these colours? What's the function of each colour within the context of the poster? There are no 'correct' answers to these questions. Encourage students to articulate their thoughts and reactions. As they constitute the main target audience of the poster, they may well associate these colours with things you had not considered.

Activity 9 You may wish to give additional prompts, such as: Can you suggest why the letter O is filled in? What's the effect of the 'framing' of the witness's face? Why is this sketched? An alternative to this activity would be to ask students to each focus on one aspect of the poster's presentation of their choosing and to write a question about it. These could then be used to stimulate further discussion.

Writing about features

Students need to be helped to develop the comments they make throughout their GCSE course if they are not to arrive at the exam equipped with little more than 'to make it stand out' or 'for effect'. The blue highlighted text indicates identification and/or description of features. Students need to know that this is a relatively low-level skill. It is the comments (pink highlighted text) that demonstrate understanding and higher-level reading skills that ultimately gain them marks in the exam. The development of relevant and perceptive comment is a key feature of later chapters in the Student Book.

Activity 10 Students are asked to copy and highlight Text C (a further paragraph of the example of student's work given in Text B), though you may prefer to distribute photocopies of this. The text is reproduced on page 15 for you. The highlighted text denotes the comments and the rest of the text is description.

> At first glance it's not clear who you are meant to imagine as 'your mate'. There is a boy hiding behind a wall, but it's only when you look closely at the framed pictures that you realise 'your mate' relates to the actual victim of the knife crime. By imagining him as 'your mate', you are being encouraged to put yourself in the position of witness to a knife crime. It is the witness, rather than the victim, who forms the visual focal point of the poster. That's because its purpose is to get you to think about what you should do if you witness a knife crime. The image of the boy is repeated three times. Each image is an enlarged copy of the previous one, with the final image showing in detail the scene reflected in the dark glasses worn by the witness. In this way, the story of what has happened is gradually revealed and forces the reader to focus on what it feels like to witness such a scene.

Activity 11 This activity requires students to put into practice what they have learned about developing comments. You may wish to collate ideas from the class in order to demonstrate how comments can be developed even further.

More about purpose and audience

k! Planning activity: Analysing an electronic text

k! Write and assess activity: Comparing non-fiction texts

The new focus on the 'Hip-Hop Opera Premiere' flyer is designed to reinforce and extend learning.

Activity 12 Students are asked to consider how the form might influence choices about content, structure and presentation. It is important for students to realise that a flyer is intended to be read in a different way from a poster. Possible answers are:

- A poster is likely to be less detailed than a flyer as its message needs to be absorbed more quickly.
- A poster may be structured more simply than a flyer, though not necessarily. The structure of the knife crime poster is quite complex. Perhaps the tendency would be to structure a poster in such a way as to make the reader curious and want to look at it again.
- A poster needs to have an immediate impact, whereas a flyer is likely to be read for its content.

You may want to follow up this discussion with a consideration of how other forms (such as leaflet, business card, advice notice) influence choices about content, structure and presentation.

Activity 13 Here further investigation of purpose and audience is encouraged. Allow students to come up with their own suggestions and priority order, providing they can support them by reference to the text. It is the explanation that is important, and the degree to which it is founded in an understanding and interpretation of content and presentation (Worksheet 2b).

Activities 14–16 Students start by working in pairs and then in groups of four. The aim is to gather ideas about the content, structure and presentation of the flyer, and use these as a basis for consideration of effectiveness. It is important that students are aware that it is perfectly acceptable for them to criticise a text, providing they can support their criticisms by reference to the text. It would be reasonable for a student to argue that this text was too busy and less effective because of this though; alternatively, its very 'busyness' may appeal to another student.

Students can make comparisons with the Crimestoppers poster if they wish to. Alternatively, this could form the basis for further structured work after the study of comparison of texts in Chapter 9.

Stretch yourself

1. After completing Activities 14 to 16, students are given the opportunity to write a commentary on the 'Hip-Hop Opera Premiere' flyer. They should be encouraged to cover a wider range of aspects. It is worth reinforcing the point that it is developed and sustained comments that demonstrate high-level understanding and reading skills. You could ask students to highlight the elements of description and comment in their answers, just as they highlighted another student's earlier in the chapter.

2. An alternative or additional task is given which enables students to be creative while also demonstrating what they have learned about effective use of presentational features to target purpose and audience. It would be helpful if students were encouraged to produce their own commentary on their final poster in which they explain the choices they made and why they made them.

Outcomes

In this chapter your students have:

- considered the importance of purpose and audience
- examined the content, structure and presentation of two texts
- practised developing comments on features of a text
- considered the effectiveness of a text.

3 Story openings

AO focus

English AO2 Reading and English Language AO3 Studying written language.

- Explain how writers use linguistic and grammatical features to achieve effects and engage and influence the reader.

In this chapter your students will:

- examine some of the techniques used by writers in the openings of novels and the effect these have on the readers.

Additional resources

Worksheets

3a: Selecting words

Getting started

Before starting the chapter you could distribute a range of classroom readers to students, who could be working in groups, and ask them to read the opening two or three paragraphs. Follow this with a discussion of how the writers attempt to engage readers in their openings and the relative success of each. Alternatively, you can ask them to talk about any story openings they have found to be particularly effective and discuss what it was that made them effective. This would be helpful to them should they do the Stretch yourself activity at the end of the chapter.

Working through the chapter

Starting to write

Activity 1 This activity can be used to help students consider what a writer might hope to achieve in his or her opening paragraphs. It is relevant to stress that the book will have been carefully researched and planned before the opening paragraphs are written. Ideas are likely to include:

- set the scene
- introduce main characters
- 'hook' the reader.

Perspective and character

It is expected that most students will have done work on first- and third-person narratives in Key Stages 2 and 3. The opening paragraph reminds them of what is meant by first-person narrative, and some of the benefits and drawbacks of writing in the first person. Before reading this paragraph you may wish to draw on students' prior learning by collating their thoughts on what is meant by writing in the first person, its advantages and its drawbacks.

Students need to understand the distinction between the narrator and the writer. They often experience difficulty in this area and it needs to be constantly reinforced. A sound grasp of this will also help them to understand the use of a persona in poetry.

Activity 2 Here students are asked to consider what is revealed about the narrator in the opening paragraphs. The following answers are likely, though accept any valid, supported answer.

- Lived in Kabul; something significant happened to him in 1975 that made him what he is today.
- He feels he has done something wrong and feels troubled or even guilty about this.
- Now living in San Francisco and regards it as his home; keeps in contact with a friend, Rahim Khan, in Pakistan.

Following clues

Viewpoints activity: Effective openings to novels

Activity 3 This activity requires students to search for further clues that the writer gives concerning what will happen in the story. Encourage them to give the reasons for their answers, where appropriate. The following answers are likely, though accept any valid, supported answer.

- Rahim Khan, Hassan, Baba, the narrator.
- The writer refers to memories from his childhood in Kabul in Afghanistan. This creates the impression that the story will be set there or in Pakistan where Rahim Khan lives.
- The reference to Rahim Khan's words, that there is 'a way to be good again', makes you think that the narrator will put right the wrong he has done.

There is further work on following clues later in the chapter.

Using language to convey meaning

Learning activity: Word choices 1

Learning activity: Word choices 2

Analysis activity: Story openings

An alternative way of using the example given would be to put the sentence on the whiteboard

Chapter 3
Story openings

and draw on students' ideas to annotate the words 'frigid' and 'overcast' accordingly. Help students to recognise that the writer chose these words, as opposed to others, deliberately and in order to affect the reader. Appropriate selection of vocabulary plays an important part in the development of the students' writing skills. It may be helpful to reinforce the need to transfer what they learn in reading to their writing.

Activity 4 Here students are required to consider what is suggested by the use of the words 'crouching', 'peeking' and 'claws' (Worksheet 3a). Below are some possible answers, though accept any valid choices.

Word chosen	Alternative word choices	What the chosen word suggests or implies
crouching	• hiding • sitting	bending uncomfortably and perhaps fearfully
peeking	• looking • staring	glancing quickly or secretively
claws	• finds • makes	with difficulty and painfully

Activity 5 This activity presents a contrast to the previous extracts in terms of mood. Students are likely to identify the happiness and sense of freedom created by the phrases 'soaring in the sky', 'danced high' and 'floating side by side'. You may also wish to explore:

- the contrast between the use of 'glanced' here and 'peeking' in the earlier extract
- the image 'like a pair of eyes', which may suggest that the writer is being watched, perhaps to reinforce the idea that he cannot escape his past.

Mood and tone are explored in more detail later in the chapter.

Character revealed through speech

Students are reminded of what is meant by third-person narrative. You may wish to draw on students' prior knowledge in order to consider the advantages and drawbacks of adopting a third-person narrative. You could also draw students' attention to the possibility of writing in the second person, though this is not a focus of this chapter.

Activities 6–8 Before completing these activities, you could ask students to work in groups of three, with one person in the role of narrator, one as Mrs Bennet and one as Mr Bennet. They should read the passage through silently, making decisions about how it should be read, before doing a group reading. Follow-up discussion, regarding how they decided to read their parts, could give useful insights into how you learn about a character through what they say and how they say it.

These three activities could be done orally, drawing on students' perceptions of the characters and recording their points on the board. Allow students freedom in the answers they give, but ensure they support their observations with evidence from the text.

With more able students you may wish to focus on the following three short sentences and what is implied by them:

- 'Mr Bennet replied that he had not.'
- 'Mr Bennet made no answer.'
- 'This was invitation enough.'

Writer's viewpoint

In this section students are required to develop their skills in identifying clues in the text and to draw deductions from these.

Activity 9 This could be done orally with answers to (a) and (b) being collated on the board and used to guide answers to (c). Accept any answers students give, providing they are supported by reference to the text.

Activity 10 This is designed to extend students' understanding of irony. Possible examples include:

- 'It is a truth universally acknowledged, that a single man in possession of a good fortune must be in want of a wife.'
- 'This was invitation enough.'

Identifying tone

Refer back to the work done on the creation of mood through the use of words in Activity 5. Another way of explaining tone and mood to students is through the use of a paint colour chart. They can see the variations in colour (just as there are variations in the tone used by a writer) and can conclude that the differing tones produce different moods.

Activity 11 Here students are required to identify linguistic and grammatical features used to create tone. The correct answers are:

1 **b** Writes in the present tense to create a sense of immediacy.

2 **d** Addresses the reader directly to place you there and help you picture what it is like.

3 **f** Uses simple adjectives sparsely to create a sense of a barren environment.

17

4 **a** Uses sarcasm to emphasise the obvious.

5 **e** Uses short paragraphs to punctuate the detail for emphasis and to make it sound very matter of fact.

6 **c** Uses simple sentence structures to emphasise each point.

7 **g** Uses sarcasm to show that something is ridiculous.

Activity 12 There are many possible answers here. Some examples are:

- **Use of sarcasm:** 'Being bitten by a scorpion or even a rattlesnake is not the worst thing that can happen to you. You won't die. Usually.'
- **Addressing the reader directly:** 'if you don't bother them, they won't bother you.' 'But you don't want to be bitten by a yellow-spotted lizard.'
- **Short paragraphs to punctuate the detail for emphasis:** 'Usually', 'Always', 'There is nothing anyone can do to you anymore.'
- **Short sentences to emphasise each point:** 'There is no lake at Camp Green Lake.' 'You won't die.'

This activity is best done orally, drawing on what the students have worked out from their analysis of the use of language in the text. Collate students' viewpoints on the board, ensuring they give reasons to explain their views.

Activity 13 This is an opportunity for students to use what they have learned from the previous activities to help them write a coherent answer to the given question. Prior to them doing this, you may wish to collate and display some of their responses to Activities 11 and 12. They should aim to write about three paragraphs and should refer to details in the text to support the things they say. At the end of writing, you could ask them to highlight all references to the text.

Examining the three openings together

Speaking and listening This activity offers students the opportunity to review the three openings in the light of what they have learned in the chapter. The prompts are offered as starting points for discussion. Students can keep their own notes or elect one member of the group to do so on their behalf.

Activity 14 This requires a written or spoken response. Remind students that this response should contain specific references to the writer's techniques as well as to content.

Stretch yourself

A suggestion for a starter activity was that students spoke about openings of stories that they had found effective. They could now focus on the techniques used by their selected writer, drawing on what they have learned in this chapter. Alternatively, you could choose a specific opening, matched to the ability of the students you are teaching, and set this task as a homework. The opening of a Dickens novel, such as *A Tale of Two Cities*, would provide a demanding stimulus for the most able students.

Outcomes

In this chapter your students have:

- considered the role of the narrator
- detected clues in a text
- examined writers' use of words for effect
- thought about the writer's viewpoint
- explored how writers present characters and create tone.

4 Judging the evidence

AO focus

English AO2 Reading and English Language AO3 Studying written language.

- Evaluate how writers use linguistic, grammatical, structural and presentational features to achieve effects and engage and influence the reader.

In this chapter your students will:

- learn about evaluation
- study two texts
- use what they have learned in Chapters 2 and 3 to help them evaluate the effectiveness of two texts.

Additional resources

Worksheets

4a: Evaluation 1
4b: Evaluation 2
4c: Analysing an example answer

Getting started

Here students learn the skills of evaluation. This chapter follows on naturally from Chapters 2 and 3, and they will be expected to apply what they have learned in those chapters when evaluating two new texts. If it is some time since they studied those chapters, you may wish to remind them of their content before starting here.

Before starting the chapter, ask students to work in pairs or groups of three and discuss how they make decisions about buying clothes and/or other items they buy – for example, computer games or mobile phones. Why would they choose one item rather than another similar one? What are the factors they take into consideration? For example, for clothes, factors may include:

- price
- durability
- suitability for a particular occasion
- fashion
- comfort
- fit.

Ask them to prioritise the factors they identify.

Explain that, in making judgements on certain factors, they are evaluating the qualities of the items in order to make an informed choice.

Working through the chapter

What does evaluate mean?

(k!) Learning activity: Analysing an online newspaper 1

(k!) Learning activity: Analysing an online newspaper 2

This section takes students through the stages of evaluation with regard to the significant features of a specific text.

By considering features of structure, presentation and language in a text, students can be helped to:

- accurately identify its intended purpose(s) and audience(s)
- support their judgements on purpose(s) and audience(s) with reference to textual detail.

Activity 1 Students can, but do not have to, present their findings in tabulated form. Possible findings are included in the table at the bottom of the page.

You may want to collate students' ideas on structure, presentation and language before they move on. Where appropriate, encourage them to explain their observations in more detail (Worksheet 4a).

Activity 2 Students are likely to identify main intended purpose(s) as being to inform and to persuade, and main audience(s) as being young people and those who want to find out more about social iPhone options. Allow other answers if supported by relevant evidence.

Structure	Presentational features	Language
- background photographs - iPhone prominently set to right and overlapping text - heading set above written text and drawing the reader's eye to the iPhone	- use of colour to separate photographs - all photographs of young people - faces in background look sad - faces on iPhone look happy	- directly addresses the reader (e.g. 'you', 'your') - colloquial language (e.g. 'mates', 'best buddies', 'the skinny') - friendly, informal tone

Having identified a wide range of features, the next stage is to consider their effects. It is important that students be allowed to develop their own ideas to texts, providing they use valid supporting evidence. It is also important that they base their comments on the effectiveness of the features and not on the product or idea that is being promoted.

Activity 3 If you collated ideas from Activity 1, you may direct students to choose from the collated list of features. Remind them of learning from Chapters 2 and 3: that it is the comment rather than the identification of the feature that demonstrates understanding of its use and a higher-level reading skill. The emphasis is always on moving students away from simply listing features and compelling them to think about reasons for the use of the features and their effects on the reader (Worksheet 4b).

The next step is for students to make judgements on the effectiveness of the features, in response to a specific question. Students often lack confidence in their own judgement and are eager to know the 'right' answer. It is important to stress that there is no 'right' answer – only relevant judgements made on evidence in the text.

Activity 4 The annotated response demonstrates the various elements of the response. You may wish to do this as a matching activity, getting students to match the elements to the response.

Activity 5 Students are now required to independently match the annotations to particular features (Worksheet 4c). They can record their findings in table form. Alternatively, if photocopies of the extract were made available to them, they could annotate these. Some of the things students might annotate are in the table below.

Feature	Example from student's writing
Links text to intended purpose	The writer uses language to persuade the reader.
Links text to intended purpose; identifies use of words	Exaggerated phrases, such as 'has never been easier' and 'Everyone's on an online social network these days', are there to make the reader think they could try it too.
Identifies use of words	The words address the reader directly with phrases such as 'Now you can exchange …'
Makes a judgement	This method would probably be successful
Links text to intended audience; identifies use of words; comments on features; supports comments with details from the text	in that it would encourage the reader to have a go. Informal language is used to target the teenage reader directly with phrases such as 'best buddies' and 'give you the skinny'.
Makes a judgement	These might make the reader more interested, though some people might prefer a less chatty and more practical approach.
Uses discursive marker to link ideas	It's only at the end of the two paragraphs that you find out what the article that follows is going to be about, probably because
Identifies feature of structure	the writer wants to hook you in first, though, personally,
Supports judgement with reasons	I think this should have come earlier. Some people might have stopped reading before they get to this bit.
Uses discursive marker to link ideas	Overall,
Makes a judgement	the text works well, with the images enhancing the message of the writing that life is better if you social network.
Identifies feature of presentation; supports judgement with reasons	I like the way moody colours are used for the background faces and the way the sad expressions contrast with the happy faces on the iPhone.
Uses discursive marker to link ideas	However,
Offers alternative view; supports alternative view with reference to the text	I think this would have been more effective if they'd used the same teenagers for both sets of pictures, suggesting that now they are networking they are much happier. This would have helped to make the meaning clearer and consequently had more effect on the reader.

Chapter 4
Judging the evidence

Writing your own evaluation

🔑 Planning activity: A comparison of two climate change websites

🔑 Planning activity: A comparison of two education websites

As you will be aware, many students find it difficult to write an evaluation. Having read and examined the features of a written evaluation, they now need practice in writing their own, drawing on what they have learned in the chapter so far.

Activity 6 This activity replicates, in brief, Activities 1–3. It enables students to prepare their ideas in advance of writing. You might like to collate their findings to (a) and (b) before they move on to (c) and the writing of their evaluation. Possible findings are:

Structure
- two sections, with photographs forming a band at the top and a central feature on Facebook with the iPhone centrally placed
- blocked information used as annotation of the central iPhone
- title 'Facebook' placed prominently overlapping top band and main section.

Presentational features
- photographs of different people
- range of colours
- heading and subheadings
- information placed in blocked sections
- illustration of iPhone showing Facebook
- range of font sizes and colours.

Language
- inclusive (for example, 'no longer restricted', 'anyone over the age of 13 can join')
- addresses reader directly (for example, 'you', 'your', 'you'll')
- colloquial language (for example, 'the lowdown on')
- tone – friendly and informal.

Intended purposes
- to inform
- to instruct
- to persuade.

Intended audiences
- young people
- people wanting to find out more about Facebook.

Students can do part (c) independently or work in pairs or small groups. Working together will help them to consider alternative viewpoints in their writing. Additionally, you may want to collate ideas or instigate class discussion on points where you have noted significant differences of opinion.

Activity 7 Students are encouraged to look back at Activity 5 before starting to write their answer. They are also provided with an outline plan which, if they choose to use it, will help them structure their ideas. You could also display a list of words and phrases that would help them to express their opinions in writing. This could include: 'I think', 'it would seem', 'because', 'this suggests that', 'suggesting', 'implying', 'would probably', 'might make/encourage', 'however', 'it seems as though'.

Activity 8 Students are asked to highlight and annotate their writing to ensure they have fulfilled the requirements of writing an evaluation. Alternatively, they could work in pairs, highlighting and annotating each other's answer. If the latter route is taken, students should be encouraged to write a summative comment at the end of the writing, indicating achievements and new targets.

While there is no Stretch yourself activity in this chapter, students do need plenty of practice at developing skills in evaluation throughout their GCSE course. You could apply the structure of Activities 6–8 to any non-fiction media text of your choosing at any time, either as a homework or as a class-based activity. It is important to remind students that it is the text and not the product that is being evaluated. This is particularly relevant if theme park leaflets are used, where students can make the mistake of talking about the appeal of the place to them, rather than the effectiveness of the leaflet with regard to its intended purpose(s) and audience(s).

In addition to this, the ability to evaluate and support judgements is a necessary skill in the study of GCSE English Literature and in many other subject areas, as well as in life in general. You could raise discussion about where students currently need to use the skill of evaluation and where they may need to in the future.

An interesting activity for group discussion is to present students with a range of holiday brochures from which they have to select the most appropriate holiday for different specified family groups, for example:

- two parents and two young children
- one parent and two teenage children
- two grandparents and two teenage grandchildren.

Further conditions could be applied, such as:

- cost restrictions
- the need for self-catering/hotel accommodation.

This activity requires students to study the brochures closely and make appropriate judgements based on the available evidence.

Students should be made aware that the skills they are developing in evaluation can be transferred to their studies elsewhere and to the choices they need to make in life.

Outcomes

In this chapter your students have:

- applied what they have learned about structure, presentation and language to two texts
- studied features of a written evaluation
- written their own evaluation of a text.

5 Texts in contexts

AO focus

English AO2 Reading.

- Understand texts in their social, cultural and historical contexts.

In this chapter your students will:

- consider how language changes over time
- explain why some writers choose to write in dialect
- learn about texts in their cultural, social and historical contexts.

Getting started

Students often know much more about the context of language than they realise and it is good for their confidence to make them aware of this. To draw on this knowledge you could put the following lines (or similar) up on the board, without the source.

> Sweet soul, let's in, and there expect their coming.
> And yet no matter; why should we go in?
> My friend Stephano, signify, I pray you,
> Within the house, your mistress is at hand;
> And bring your music forth into the air.
>
> William Shakespeare, *Merchant of Venice* (V.i)

Ask them to identify who they think wrote these lines and to give their reasons for their choice. You could draw their attention to particular phrases such as 'and there expect their coming', 'Within the house' and 'bring your music forth into the air', and discuss modern-day equivalents of these. Collate their ideas on the board before confirming, or revealing, Shakespeare as the author.

Working through the chapter

Texts in time

As students may have seen in the starter activity, modern English is not the same as in the past. Students sometimes approach Shakespeare as though he were writing in a different language that needs to be 'translated'. They need to understand that all languages change and that the language they use today will be as unfamiliar to students in 400 years as Shakespeare's language is to them.

Activity 1 The texts are written by poets separated by 600 years. The aim of the activity is, first, to get students to use their knowledge of English to work out the meaning of the Chaucerian extract. Allow them time to try to identify the words and their meanings and to share their ideas with other students. The second aim of the activity is to help them realise that Chaucer would have as much difficulty in understanding a 21st-century text as they have with his. They will probably realise that Chaucer would not understand the references to 'the mobile', 'the landline phones', 'guns', 'the phone', 'Last Chance Saloon', 'Sheriff', 'text', 'silver bullets', and would be unlikely to be able to make much sense of the poem because of this. The Duffy poem appears in the *AQA Anthology* and this activity also acts as a helpful introduction to it.

Texts in dialect

Viewpoints activity: The social context of a novel

It is likely that most students will already know some of the differences between dialect and Standard English, and this is covered in more detail in Chapters 14 and 25 of the Student Book.

Activity 2 This is designed to remind students of relatively well-known dialects:

- Australian (Aussie)
- Liverpudlian (Scouse)
- Yorkshire/Lancashire/Durham (Northern)
- Newcastle upon Tyne (Geordie)
- London (Cockney).

They are also asked to consider examples of dialect in the media. Soaps such as *EastEnders*, *Emmerdale* and *Coronation Street* can provide a useful starting point for discussion.

When identifying examples of dialect that students or those in the area they live in might use, it would be helpful to collate their examples on the board.

Activity 3

a Students are likely to identify the Scottish dialect in the first extract and the Jamaican or West Indian dialect in the second. This is a good opportunity to explore how they know this and to draw out their experiences of hearing/reading dialects. Allow them to experiment with working out meaning and to exchange ideas between pairs.

b There are no 'correct' reasons, but here are some possible student suggestions:

- they are writing for a small local audience
- they want to be different

English and English Language Teacher's Book Higher Tier
Section A: Reading

- they want to show their pride in where they are from
- they want to promote the use of dialects in writing
- they don't know how to write in Standard English.

You could collate their ideas and decide the most likely explanation(s) for Burns and Bennett choosing to write in dialect.

Texts and culture

This section aims to help students recognise that all texts have a cultural context.

Activity 4 Writers often assume knowledge of cultural context in their readers. This activity encourages students to consider how much of this knowledge is taken for granted by the writer. Students are often encouraged to read texts from different cultures, but need to understand that to others their culture is 'different'.

Activity 5 This is an opportunity for students to identify features of the culture of the area in which they live. You could develop this further by asking them to identify features of cultures within that culture, for example, different racial groups or different social groups. Much will depend on the area in which you teach and your students' experience of a range of cultures within that area, though it is likely that they will all be able to identify features of specific teenage groups such as Goths and Emos.

Their written paragraphs introducing a stranger to the 'culture of their area' might form a very interesting class display.

Context

k! Planning activity: Responding to a pre-20th century text

k! Analysis activity: Analysing texts from other cultures

Students need to show that they understand texts in their social, cultural and historical contexts. Too often when writing about texts, students simply have a stand-alone opening or add-on paragraph which explains these contexts. This is of little value. They need to be helped to use the context to develop and then demonstrate their understanding of the text.

In this section of the chapter they read and form an understanding of the poem 'Futility' without any given context. The illustration that accompanies the poem is intentionally neutral and provides a point for consideration later in Activity 9. Having considered the poem without any contextual detail, they then reconsider the poem in the light of its social and historical context.

Activity 6 The following are examples of the answers students might give:

1. Probably a farmer (fields unsown).
2. He can't be woken up even by the sun which always used to wake him.
3. Sad, gentle, quiet, sorrowful.
4. Why should it be so difficult to bring him back to life? What was the point in him being born and growing? What's the point in the sun making anything grow?
5. Angry, questioning, upset.
6. That it's a waste of a life; that there is no point to it.
7. 'Futility' suggests that something is pointless or has a lack of meaning.
8. How so much goes into a life and how easily it can be destroyed; how there is no point to living when it can end so quickly; sad, unhappy, reflective.

Having responded to the poem in Activity 6, students now learn about its historical and social context, alongside biographical details about Wilfred Owen.

Activity 7 This aims to encourage students to use their contextual knowledge to develop their understanding of, and response to, the poem. You may wish to deal with the bullet points through general class discussion. Below are just some of the points that might be made:

- The man is probably a soldier and has died in battle or from battle wounds – he was probably fighting in France during the First World War. He might be a young man.
- There's sadness in the first stanza and maybe bitterness in the second stanza – it's as though the first stanza is about the death and the second one about the stupidity of such a death.
- He seems to feel very sad that so much effort has gone into this man's growing and yet it's been destroyed so easily.
- He appears to feel angry about the war and as though the death of this man is pointless and not achieving anything. There may be a suggestion that war goes against natural things as even the sun cannot wake the dead man.
- The word 'futility', which suggests that something is of no use or wasted, seems to sum up the poem's feelings about this young man's death and, perhaps, about the war in general.

Activity 8 This is intended to be a short piece of writing in which students reconsider their answer to the final question in Activity 6, taking into account what they have since discovered about the poem.

Activity 9 Poems create pictures in the mind of the reader. The picture used alongside 'Futility' gives no indication of war. Now that students know the background to this poem, and have reconsidered their response in the light of that, they are asked to consider the appropriateness of the picture and whether a different image would be better.

More about context

Activity 10 Here students are invited to consider 'The Soldier'. The focus is on the attitude to war that it presents and how this contrasts with that presented in 'Futility', written just a few years later. You may prefer to read the poem aloud and discuss its implications as a class.

Activity 11 Likely answers include:

a For the general public; as propaganda; for soldiers about to go to war.

b That if he dies in battle, his sacrifice and the place where he fell would belong to England. It is a very patriotic poem, suggesting that everything he is is due to his life in England.

c Gentle, peaceful, accepting, reassuring.

d Comforted; proud to be English; reassured that the war was noble and worthwhile.

Activity 12 This could be done through class discussion. You might want to point out similarities between the poems, as well as their essential difference. Points might include:

- Both refer to England in a positive way.
- Both refer to death in a foreign country.
- 'The Soldier' promotes the view that it is honourable to die for one's country; 'Futility' suggests that it is a waste of life and that there is no point to it.

Stretch yourself

This activity gives students the opportunity to write within a specific context, where knowledge of the subject matter is assumed. You could distribute photocopies of a current news article as a stimulus for writing. With able students you might like to encourage them, after writing, to explore the different ways in which their work would be understood by people who did or did not have the contextual knowledge.

Consideration of texts in their contexts is also a feature of the study of GCSE English Literature; you might like to draw your students' attention to this by showing the relevant Literature AO:

- **AO4:** Relate texts to their social, cultural and historical contexts; explain how texts have been influential and significant to self and other readers in different contexts and at different times.

Outcomes

In this chapter your students have:

- considered how language changes over time
- examined the use of dialect in two extracts
- learnt about the cultural, social and historical contexts of texts.

6 A twist in the tale

AO focus

English AO2 Reading and English Language AO3 Studying written language.

- Explain how writers use linguistic and structural features to achieve effects and engage and influence the reader.
- Develop and sustain interpretations of writer's ideas and perspectives.

In this chapter your students will:

- consider how stories are structured to achieve particular effects
- examine how writers manipulate readers
- think about how a character is created
- develop their ideas beyond a text.

Additional resources

Worksheets

6a: Get the story straight

Getting started

A useful starter activity would be to work through the 'Using a dictionary' section of the English essentials chapter on pages 216–17 of the Student Book. This links directly with the opening section of this chapter, which reinforces the usefulness of reference to a dictionary for meaning.

Alternatively, you could invite one or two students to tell the class a story. It could be true or fictional. For each story told, you could identify positive key features, such as the setting of the scene, the order in which the events were narrated (chronological or otherwise), the ways in which the narrator held the audience's attention, the conclusion.

Working through the chapter

Using a dictionary

This section explores the meaning of the word 'narrate' and throws light on how to use the words 'narrative', 'narration' and 'narrator'. These are all terms commonly used in the study of English. Aim to help students understand that in fiction the 'narrator' does not necessarily speak for the author, reinforcing ideas covered in the opening section of Chapter 3. You may also want to introduce the idea of a 'persona' (an assumed identity or character).

Activity 1

a The 'rate' part.
b A recounting of events; the subject of a narrative.
c A narrator.
d Latin.

A reader's expectations

Viewpoints activity: Making predictions

Before starting this section you may want to explore students' experiences of fables and other short stories with a moral tale: fairy tales are a useful source, where good almost always prevails over evil. If you have students from a range of cultures there is an opportunity to consider the common elements of such stories from very different parts of the world.

Activity 2 This is designed to help students appreciate that writers consciously control their readers' expectations. It would be advisable to insist that students answer each question before reading on. Alternatively, you could present the story in stages with the related question(s), using a whiteboard.

There are no 'correct' answers to these questions. Their intention is to make the reader stop and work out how the writer is manipulating their expectations. Once students have written their answers you might want to discuss their observations.

Narrative structure

It is likely that students will be familiar with the term 'chronological order', though it is worth checking their understanding before proceeding.

Activity 3 (Worksheet 6a) The correct chronological order is:

f, b, c, d, e, l, i, j, k, m, a, g, h

Manipulating the reader's expectations

Analysis activity: The writer's intention

This section looks more closely at how a writer manipulates a reader's expectations. By closely analysing various stages of the story, with its corresponding shifts in tone and plot, the student gains insight into the motivation and skill of the writer. The ability to manipulate the reader's expectations is also a key writing skill and students should be encouraged to transfer learning into their own writing.

Activity 4 The following answers indicate some of the things your students might say. You may wish to point these out to students should you go through the questions orally rather than asking them to review each other's answers. This would be useful preparation for the written task.

a   At first the mood seems peaceful, with the quiet of the room and the dimness of the early evening. However, this is in contrast to the mood of Graham – he is unsettled by thoughts of his mentally arrested son.

b   It is clear that Graham loves and values his son, but the suggestion that the child will not grow up to leave him makes the reader think that maybe this will not be the case and he will lose the child he loves so much.

c   The doorbell ringing disturbs Graham's flow of thought, but also the mood of the passage. The peace and quiet is broken. The shortness of the sentence serves to emphasise this disturbance and shift in the plot.

d   The writer suggests there is nothing particularly notable about Niemand. He seems insignificant. However, the fact that Graham thinks he is 'obviously harmless' makes the reader suspect that this may not be the case and that he will in fact prove to be harmful.

e   The impression of Graham so far has been of a quiet, thoughtful man who cares greatly for his handicapped son. Here we find out more about his work and that, in the view of his visitor, it threatens the future of mankind. As well as his caring side, we are now aware of a much more dangerous one.

f   Niemand's reaction to the boy seems genuine. He is not embarrassed by his presence and relates appropriately to the boy's mental age. He says he likes him and there is sincerity in the way he says it. All these things make the reader feel it is unlikely that Niemand will harm Harry.

g   Graham acknowledges that his work could result in the destruction of mankind, but he is not concerned by this. He sees his work from a personal perspective only. The fact that he is only concerned with the progression of science makes him seem selfish and not deserving of sympathy.

h   It is important that the reader does not know what has happened. This information is withheld until the end of the story. The reader is left imagining what has occurred in the room.

i   The reader knows Niemand has been into Harry's room and now starts to feel anxious about the nature of the 'gift', especially as Niemand says, 'I hope you'll forgive me'. As Graham walks into Harry's room we are expecting something bad to have happened. The interruption of Graham's speech reinforces this expectation, as does the 'sudden sweat on his forehead'. By the end of these lines the reader still does not know what the 'it' is.

j   On the surface, the reader is forced to agree with Graham. Harry is mentally arrested and could easily have shot himself while playing with the gun. But then we think again. Why did Niemand give Harry the gun? The reader realises that it parallels Graham's own actions: he is giving a weapon to mankind and mankind is likened to Harry – not capable of handling it. The unanswered question at the end of the story is: Will Graham realise this?

Activity 5 If students have completed Activity 4 on their own, they now have the opportunity to compare, discuss and, where appropriate, amend their answers.

Activity 6 This activity draws on students' learning from Activities 4–5, requiring students to develop their ideas in a sustained written response. It might be useful to set a time limit of 20 minutes or thereabouts, with the suggestion to write three or four developed paragraphs.

Examining a character

Planning activity: Examining a character

This section focuses on how a writer develops a character, and in focusing on inconsistencies encourages students to explore beyond the surface detail. In doing so they are developing their skills in inference and deduction.

Activity 7 Students could work in pairs or individually. Encourage them to choose their own form of note-making. It is likely that they will include the following ideas (and others) in their notes:

- **Appearance:** small, nondescript, harmless-looking.
- **Words:** polite, seems knowledgeable, wise? Appears to make a valid point about Graham's work, concerned about the future of mankind.
- **Actions:** disturbs Graham at home in the evening – suggests some urgency in visit; body language and tone of voice suggest concern is genuine (for example, 'interlocked his fingers', 'with obvious sincerity'); friendly and kind manner when speaking to Harry.

- **Inconsistencies:** more assertive than appearance suggests; kind to Harry and yet leaves a loaded revolver with him – prepared to risk the boy's life to make his point; had clearly planned in advance what he would do should Graham ignore his warning.

Developing your response to a character

You could collate students' ideas and then move the discussion on to consideration of the wider questions raised in the subsequent four bullet points. In discussion, these questions could be applied to both Niemand and Graham. The information that the word 'niemand' is German for 'no one' or 'nobody' should create some opportunities for discussion of symbolic significance.

Activity 8 Students could extend their notes during and/or after discussion of the bullet points. The success of the activity depends on the sharing of ideas where more able students can lead others into deeper exploration of meaning and association.

Developing and sustaining interpretation

Able readers use what they read to stimulate their thinking processes. Students need to be encouraged to engage with the wider implications of a text: to bring their ideas and knowledge to a text and to use ideas from a text to help them to understand and interpret things beyond it.

Speaking and listening This activity is designed to help students apply their thinking about the ideas in 'The Weapon' to other areas.

You could ask students to undertake further research about Hiroshima and Nagasaki, or the Pacific tests in the 1950s, or cloning and/or genetic engineering before doing the speaking and listening activity. Groups could also present their conclusions to the rest of the class, leading to a more general class discussion.

The fact that Brown wrote 'The Weapon' in 1951 is not insignificant and could be used to reinforce learning in Chapter 5 on historical and cultural contexts.

Stretch yourself
Depending on time, you may wish to set a word limit on this. A fable, in the manner of Aesop's, should be no more than 200 words. However, if time permits, the limit for a more developed narrative could be as many as 1,000 words and the task could be set as a homework. Many students enjoy writing stories and this activity gives them the opportunity to be creative. Allow time for students to exchange, read and comment on each other's stories.

Outcomes

In this chapter your students have:

- examined the structure of a fable
- traced the chronological order in a short story
- examined how a writer manipulates a reader's expectations
- studied how a writer creates a character
- used ideas in a text to inform their own thinking beyond it.

7 Analysing argument

AO focus

English AO2 Reading and English Language AO3 Studying written language.

- Read and understand texts, selecting material appropriate to purpose.

In this chapter your students will:

- trace the development of a writer's ideas
- understand and explain the ideas expressed by writers
- make appropriate references to texts
- examine how writers use language to influence their readers.

Additional resources

Worksheets
7a: Wild Thoughts

Getting started

Before starting the chapter you may find it useful to discuss with students what they understand by the term 'writing to argue'. Although many of them will be familiar with this from their work at Key Stage 3, it is essential to establish whole-class understanding. For some students the term may mean presenting a set of one-sided arguments only. It is important to stress that when presenting a point of view, a writer may see points from both sides, as in the argument they will study in this chapter.

As a starter activity, you may wish to set up a group task such as the reading of several short texts (for example, newspaper or magazine letters to the editor) asking students to identify the main points. A homework task for students could be to write their own 'writing to argue' texts, to include at least three key points. An accessible topic could be 'Homework serves no useful purpose for either teachers or students.' Following the homework task, students could be invited to highlight the key points in each other's arguments.

When following and analysing an argument it is helpful to students if they can make notes, highlight and underline on the text. With this in mind, it would be useful to make a separate copy of Text A available to students for them to annotate as they work through the activities.

Dividing the text into three, prior to initial reading, can assist students to follow the development of ideas in a text. By reading one section at a time and asking themselves the questions below about each section, students can gain a clear grasp of how the writer's ideas are developing.

- What is this about?
- Why has the writer written this?
- How does this make the reader react?

Answers are intended to be brief. The initial reading of the text could be used as a paired reading task or as a whole-class activity before completing the activities which follow.

Working through the chapter

Identifying key points

It is important to stress that identifying key points is an essential part of following any argument. It is also useful to point out that an argument often has more than one key point as the writer's point of view is developed.

Activity 1 The following are the most likely answers:

a Paragraph 3.
b Paragraph 4.
c Paragraph 2.
d Paragraph 5.
e Paragraph 1.

If students find alternative responses when matching up the letters and paragraphs they should be encouraged to explain their thinking. They should not be made to think they have chosen the 'wrong' answer.

How writers influence their readers

Planning activity: Analysing an argument

As a pre-teaching activity you could begin this section with a revision of fact and opinion based on texts such as advertisements. Students could be asked to research texts as a homework task and to bring their own examples of fact and opinion for whole-class or small-group discussion.

Next, a general discussion of Text A, identifying examples of both fact and opinion, could be helpful. Students should be made aware of false facts and consider, for example, whether the phrase 'It's hardly ever true' is fact or opinion, and how the word 'true' can be used in a misleading way.

29

English and English Language Teacher's Book Higher Tier
Section A: Reading

Fact	Reason for use	Desired effect
The Canadian Province of British Columbia has announced plans to protect a huge swathe of Pacific Coast rainforest.	To inform the reader about the plans for the protection of the rainforest. To give them the information they need to follow the article.	To make them aware that the rainforest exists and to let them know exactly where in the world it is. To make readers aware it is an important conservation area.
It is home to everything from bald eagles and beavers to wolves and whales.	To reinforce the point that this is an area rich in wildlife.	To make readers appreciate the importance of the rainforest and to help them understand what richness of wildlife could be lost if it is not protected.
The rainforest covers an area twice the size of Belgium.	To convince readers that this is a very large area of great importance.	To make readers share his sense of awe and wonder for the enormous size of the rainforest.
The agreement does specify that any logging and mining in the area must be sustainable.	To make the reader question whether the agreement to provide sustainable logging and mining will be kept.	To get readers on his side and to make them as suspicious of the promises made in the agreement as he is. This is indicated in the final part of the sentence: '… anyone who believes that must be kidding themselves.'

Activity 2 (Worksheet 7a) There are no set answers to this activity, as students may legitimately select different reasons for use from the list. What is important is that they work out the effect on the reader. This task and the one which follows could be used as paired activities. The table above shows some likely responses.

Activity 3 (Worksheet 7a) As before, the answers are not set although some possibilities are provided in the table at the bottom of the page. Students should be encouraged to develop their own ideas about the text. Differences between answers may provide useful discussion points.

Once students have identified the opinions, you could ask them to examine the language more closely (for example, the use of colloquial language in the second example in the table below and its effect on the reader).

A follow-on activity could be to ask students to identify exactly where in the text the facts and opinions occur and to investigate the reasons for their distribution throughout the text. A copy of the text and highlighters would make this task easier.

Referring to details in the text

The examples of different methods of referring to texts given here can be used to reinforce prior learning of Key Stage 3 skills. No one method is preferable; it should be stressed that good answers use a combination of all three methods.

Activity 4 Students should write approximately 8–10 lines using one or more of the methods of referring to texts, as exemplified in the Student Book.

Opinion	Reason for use	Desired effect
It's an exhilarating place.	To persuade the reader.	To influence them towards sharing his opinion that more of the rainforest should be saved from development.
Anyone who believes that must be kidding themselves.	To make the reader question further.	To make the reader doubt whether the logging and mining activities really will be sustainable.
Our expectations are now so low that we are thankful for progress of any kind.	To give emphasis to a particular point.	This summarises for the reader his argument that conservationists are not trying hard enough to protect vulnerable areas.

Chapter 7
Analysing argument

The following points might be included:
- Plans to save part of an impartial area are good news but not enough is being done.
- He is sceptical about the decision and the failure of conservation groups to set their goals higher.

Recognising techniques

Webquest activity: How are teenagers represented in the press?

Text B can be divided into three to enable students to focus on the argument in small sections. You may ask them to read the text alone or with a partner before tackling the activities.

Before reading the article you could display the headline 'The Murder of Johnny'.

Rhetorical questions

Activity 5 Further examples of rhetorical questions and possible responses are listed in the table at the bottom of the page.

Once students have identified rhetorical questions, you may wish to explore with them the writer's purpose in including so many in a relatively short text. Possible reasons could be as follows:

- The writer feels so passionately about her subject that she wants to engage readers very directly in order to sway their opinion.
- The writer is aware that many readers may not share her point of view. In using a series of questions she is making them question their own attitudes.

Emotive use of language

Many students use the term 'emotive language'. It may be useful to point out that it is not the words that are emotive, but their intended effect on the reader. Reference to other texts could reinforce this point. Students could be asked to identify three or four examples of language used emotively and to explain their effect on the reader.

Activity 6 Here are some of the likely responses:

- 'The wildlife park was his prison ...': This suggests he was being detained unfairly – this may make readers feel angry on his behalf.
- 'People have the right to life, freedom and welfare. That is what Johnny deserved.': This makes readers agree that the rights listed are reasonable and should be expected by all. The use of the word 'deserved' makes readers believe Johnny is as entitled to these rights as any human being. Readers may feel aggrieved that he is being deprived of his rights.
- '... he was an object, an item of property ...': This is clearly the opposite of what the writer believes, she wants readers to feel it is wrong that Johnny is regarded as an object. She may also want to arouse their sympathy at the lack of respect that she perceives.

Identifying bias

You could begin by asking students what they understand by the term 'bias', with examples they have encountered of it – perhaps in a sporting context.

Activity 7 Students should be encouraged to discuss the implications of the word 'murder', which has connotations of crime and injustice. The use of a commonly used name for the chimpanzee and the effect of this on readers could also be discussed. Some may feel that the writer is deliberately misleading readers in the title.

Rhetorical questions	How and why the author is attempting to influence the reader
Surely whoever pulled the trigger was arrested, and the shooting investigated?	The writer wants readers to believe a crime has been committed.
Why this radical difference in treatment?	The writer is drawing attention to the fact that Johnny has been unjustly treated and that he would not have been treated in this way if he were a human being.
Is it because chimpanzees are not members of our biological group?	The writer is trying to make readers believe that Johnny has been discriminated against simply because he is not human.
Shouldn't we suppose that Johnny and his fellow beings are quite similar to us?	The writer wants the reader to accept the premise that there is very little difference between humans and chimpanzees. The inference is that they should be treated equally.

English and English Language Teacher's Book Higher Tier
Section A: Reading

Any unbiased title is acceptable as a replacement. For example:

- Chimpanzee escapes from wildlife park.

Activity 8 Students should recognise that in all the examples the writer is manipulating readers into thinking that chimpanzees should have the same rights as humans. The first example, in particular, makes the reader assume that Johnny is a person and not a chimpanzee. Students could be asked to identify all the words in the text that could apply equally to human beings. When asked to rewrite an unbiased version, students may need to add words or phrases.

Some suggested responses are as follows:

- **'... he lived with his friend Koko and five other companions.'**: The writer wants the reader to think that Johnny lived as any ordinary human being. The word 'friend' reveals the writer's bias. This could be rewritten as 'He shared his home with six other chimpanzees.'

- **'... he did what any of us would have done ...'**: The word 'us' implies that Johnny shared the experience and feelings of human beings. This phrase makes the reader believe Johnny did no harm at all. This phrase could be rewritten as 'he did as other animals have done before him.'

- **'... he should never have been kept prisoner in the first place.'**: The word 'never' underlines the fact that Johnny was not a danger to anyone and that he had been treated very unfairly. Students may also point out that the word 'prisoner' is not one that is usually applied to animals in zoos. This could be rewritten as 'Some people may feel that chimpanzees should not be kept in wildlife parks.'

Bringing the learning together

Activity 9 This task could be tackled with a preliminary whole-group/small-group discussion of the text and the questions before students write the answers individually. Students should make brief notes only, as the main task is the one which follows in Activity 10.

Some likely responses are:

a Main points of the argument:
  - Traffic causes many problems, such as pollution, health problems (increase in asthma) and congestion in towns and cities.
  - We should follow the example of a town in Belgium where the needs of people have priority.
  - Free public transport would have many advantages if introduced.
  - Local councils should have the courage to introduce free transport.

b

Facts	Opinions
- Traffic doubled in last 25 years. - Hundreds of local authorities break EU regulations. - Hasselt – fourth-largest town in Belgium – has introduced free public transport.	- Journey to work/school an ever-increasing nightmare. - A hassle, exhausting, etc. - Early morning misery. - A philosophy we should try to emulate. - Undeniable right to mobility. - Fume-spewing monster.

(i) Examples of language used emotively will be found within the opinions: for example, 'misery', 'exhausting'.

(ii) An example of a rhetorical question is 'why can't we?'

c Emotive language is used to convince the reader that traffic in towns is unacceptable. Rhetorical questions are used to encourage readers to accept the concept of free public transport in towns.

d Likely examples of bias are:
  - early morning misery
  - fume-spewing monster.

The bias is intended to make readers adopt a negative view of cars and traffic.

Activity 10 This activity allows students to write an essay-style response (approximately 8–12 lines) to draw all their learning together. They should be encouraged to use their notes to assist them and to use the bullet points to structure their ideas. The bullet points can also be used as guidelines for peer assessment to add further focus to the learning.

Outcomes

Analysis activity: Understanding the writer's point of view

In this chapter your students have:

- identified the key points in an argument
- learned how writers use fact and opinion to influence their readers
- used a range of methods to refer to texts
- recognised a range of techniques used by writers to influence readers
- learned how to recognise bias in a text.

8 The writer's point of view

AO focus

English AO2 Reading and English Language AO3 Studying written language.

- Develop interpretations of writers' ideas and perspectives.
- [English AO2 only] Understand texts in their social, cultural and historical contexts.

In this chapter your students will:

- read between the lines to work out the writer's ideas
- understand the background to texts
- develop comments about texts in detail.

Additional resources

Worksheets

8a: Interpreting texts

8b: Sustaining an interpretation 1

8c: Sustaining an interpretation 2

Getting started

Before starting the chapter it is important to establish students' understanding of the importance of expressing their own opinions on texts. It should be stressed that there is often no 'correct answer' in English and that they should be confident in explaining their own point of view.

As a starter activity you could provide students working in pairs with a series of statements and ask them to explore the ideas behind them before deciding whether they agree or disagree with them. Asking students to give more than one reason for their response will reinforce for them the idea that interpreting a text means exploring a response rather than providing one reason only in support of an answer. The students could then share their ideas with another pair to highlight the point that there can be a range of acceptable responses to texts.

Suggested statements:

- Having too much money can be a bad or even a dangerous thing.
- I refuse to feel guilty about what is happening to our environment; anything I could do wouldn't make any difference.
- Giving is always better than receiving.

Working through the chapter

Reading between the lines

It is important to stress to students that an interpretation of a text means that they will give their own viewpoint based on evidence from the text. Class discussion of texts wherever possible should encourage the expression of different viewpoints about them.

When teaching the interpretation of texts it can be useful to guide students towards the use of words such as 'might', 'maybe' and 'possibly', which enable them to interpret ideas rather than merely explain what is in the text already. Wherever possible, students should be encouraged to consider alternative interpretations.

Activity 1 The questions at the beginning of the text will enable students to pick up on the main gist. They are general questions and therefore may be of use in tackling any unseen text when you wish to promote active reading strategies. Sharing responses with a partner is an important feature of the task as it reinforces the idea that one student's interpretation may differ from another's.

Activity 2 The purpose of this activity is to enable students to focus more closely on the feelings and ideas in the text. It is likely that they will give similar answers to those below, but accept any valid answer supported by reference to the text. The skills the students worked on in Chapter 7 in making references to the text to support an answer should be built on at this point.

Likely answers to questions:

a How to promote a single from the new album; the text suggests that this has not been going well and that Geldof is worried about it.

b The shock and horror of what he saw in the news report changed his perspective, possibly made him realise that there were much more serious problems than promoting a single.

c Expect students to suggest that as a mother Paula was disturbed by the sight of suffering children, that it was a mother's instinct that made her want to check on her own healthy child.

d The question refers to the paragraph beginning 'The images'. Students may suggest that Geldof feels guilty that, like others, he has 'allowed' this situation to happen and also guilty that he was unaware that these things were happening. He may feel compelled to help.

e Students may suggest words such as 'shocked', 'horrified', 'guilty'. If the activity is used as an oral activity they could be asked to explain their choices.

f He is no longer focused on his own problems, but on the problem of how to help starving people in Ethiopia.

Making inferences

k! Viewpoints activity: Developing an understanding of a character

Activity 3 (Worksheet 8a) Students should be encouraged to make several suggestions for each point. Likely responses are given in the table below, but any valid responses are acceptable.

On completion of the activity, responses could be discussed in groups or as a whole class to compare different interpretations. You could also ask students to select the phrase that they felt was the most powerful or shocking, before sharing their ideas with others.

Understanding the writer's perspective

k! Write and assess activity: Facts and opinions

The activities that follow are intended to develop students' skills in making their own interpretations of texts, as well as enabling them to consider what the writer's purpose may have been.

Activity 4 This activity could be linked with Speaking and listening activities, either as practice in the skills required for Discussing and listening or as part of an individual or joint presentation after the research task referred to below.

Here students are invited to explore the social, historical and cultural aspects of a text. As an extension/homework task they could be encouraged to undertake further research into the life and works of Tennyson/and or the background to the Battle of Balaclava.

Students should be encouraged to read the text aloud and to discuss their response to the writer's use of rhyme and rhythm. You may wish to develop this further by focusing on the following questions:

- Find examples of rhyme in the poem. What does the use of rhyme add to the poem?
- At what points in the poem is the rhythm most pronounced? What does the rhythm remind you of?

You may also wish to ask students to present a reading of some or all of the poem, experimenting with different volume and tone of voice and sound effects.

Developing an interpretation

k! Planning activity: The writer's perspective

Activity 5 You may wish to ask students to make notes on each of the statements before they discuss their opinions with other students. There are opportunities here for applying these statements to other poems from the conflict section of the *AQA Anthology* and for creating a classroom

Evidence from the text	Interpretation
There was horror on a monumental scale.	This makes me think something terrible had happened. It suggests Geldof was extremely shocked by what he saw. The word 'monumental' emphasises his reaction, implying the horror was on a scale not seen before.
People so shrunken by starvation they looked like people from another planet.	Underlines the extreme scale of their hunger. Presents a very stark picture of the effects of the famine. Helps reader understand the impact of the news report on Geldof.
The camera … occasionally dwelling on one person so that he looked directly at me, sitting comfortably in my living room.	Produces feeling of guilt in Geldof. Makes him feel compelled to act. May also make reader respond in the same way.
All around was the murmur of death like a hoarse whisper or the buzzing of flies.	By appealing to sense of hearing makes the situation seem even more appalling. The buzzing of flies may make reader think of how flies would buzz around a body after death. Underlines the hopelessness of the situation.
A tragedy the world had contrived not to notice.	Suggests we are too comfortable in our own world to take action – preferable to ignore the famine. Almost an accusation.

Chapter 8
The writer's point of view

noticeboard with students' comments as they work through the poems.

Activity 6 In this activity students should focus on individual words and phrases in order to work out the writer's point of view (Worksheet 8a).

The following are possible interpretations:

Evidence from the text	Interpretation
Boldly they rode and well	The word 'boldly' suggests he admires their bravery. This is backed up by the word 'well'.
They that had fought so well	The repetition of the word 'well' emphasises his admiration for their bravery.
Noble six hundred!	The word 'noble' implies that he looks up to them and has great respect for their deeds in battle.

Developing and sustaining an interpretation

Activity 7 (Worksheet 8b) It should be pointed out that the student who wrote Text C makes simple comments on the text but does not extend them. The response of the student in Text D extends comments to sustain the interpretation:

- identified the poet's point of view – 'admires'; 'is praising'
- referred to the text – any of the quotations
- developed/sustained comments – the first three-and-a-half lines
- made corrections – 'their courage is again emphasised ...'

Activity 8 (Worksheet 8c) Quotations that the students could use to illustrate the horrific conditions of the battle are as follows:

- 'Cannon to the right of them ... Volley'd and thunder'd'
- 'Storm'd at with shot and shell'
- 'Into the jaws of Death ...'

Students who read the text carefully will note that the lines 'Reel'd from the sabre stroke/ Shatter'd and sunder'd' refer to the enemy soldiers, but nevertheless show what the conditions of battle were like.

Students should be reminded that it is their own point of view that counts. They should be encouraged to offer their own interpretations by making several comments on each quotation selected.

It may be helpful to some students to provide them with sentence starters that will assist them in explaining the impact of words and phrases on the reader. For example:

- 'This suggests ...'
- 'This implies ...'
- 'This makes the reader think ...'

Activity 9

a Likely response is that the word 'blunder'd' implies a stupid mistake and suggests he was very dismissive of the commanders/had no respect for them.

b The lines suggest the soldiers were obedient as good soldiers should be/were victims who died while carrying out their duty. Repetition emphasises the mistake made by the commanders and the soldiers' sense of duty.

c Students should be encouraged to explain their own response to the personification in 'jaws' and 'mouth', and to explain the effect of the repetition of the word 'Hell'.

> **Review and reflect**
>
> This activity is intended to give students the opportunity to put into practice all they have learned so far in the chapter. You may want to remind them that they must be confident in expressing their own point of view about texts and in making extended comments.

Stretch yourself

This is intended as an extension activity for more able students. They would benefit from some background research into contemporary reports of the Battle of Balaclava before undertaking it. This activity has potential for linking with the Speaking and listening role-play task, either to teach the skills or as part of the controlled assessment task.

Outcomes

In this chapter your students have:

- selected a range of details from texts
- interpreted the writers' meaning based on evidence in the text
- developed their comments in detail.

9 Alternative interpretations

AO focus

English AO2 Reading and English Language AO3 Studying written language.

- Develop and sustain interpretations of writers' ideas and perspectives.
- [English AO2 only] Understand texts in their social, cultural and historical contexts.

In this chapter your students will:

- extend their skills in interpreting the writers' ideas and perspectives in texts
- express their own opinions on texts
- offer alternative interpretations of texts.

Additional resources

Worksheets

9a: Interpreting the writer's ideas
9b: Your personal response

Getting started

The purpose of this chapter is to provide opportunities for students at the upper end of the ability range to extend their skills in interpreting texts, exploring alternative interpretations and writing full and detailed responses.

It may be useful for students to read and discuss 'War Photographer' by Carol Ann Duffy before reading the text by Don McCullin, as there is an overlap between the themes and ideas in the poem and McCullin's account in the Student Book. Once the prose text has been studied, you could ask students to look back at the poem and draw up their own list of comparisons. The following background information may be useful.

The poem 'War Photographer' was written at a time when Carol Ann Duffy was friendly with Don McCullin. She said about the poem: 'I'm interested in the photographer, in the dilemma of someone who has that as a job.'

As a homework or extended research task you could ask students to research further into the friendship between McCullin and Duffy and into McCullin's work as a photographer.

Areas in the poem for students to explore in groups or with a partner could be:

- how the poem draws a contrast between life in rural England and the war zones photographed by the photographer
- how the poem focuses on the suffering of two individuals
- how the photographer may feel about his work with particular reference to the first and last stanzas.

Working through the chapter

Begin by asking students what they remember about how to write an interpretation of a text based on the work they did in Chapter 8.

Interpreting the writer's ideas

k! Viewpoints activity: Forming an impression

Activity 1 Students could answer the questions independently before sharing their responses with another student (Worksheet 9a). The aim of this is to reinforce the idea that some texts can have a range of different interpretations. After the partner task you could coordinate ideas in a whole-class plenary.

Teacher questioning plays a very important part in developing the skills of interpretation, as students often articulate the beginning of an idea but need further encouragement in the form of questions to follow it to a conclusion.

Possible answers:

a The writer may wish to make a comparison between the rural idyll of birdsong and rolling hills and the noise of dive-bombing aircraft. The implicit message about war is that it disturbs the natural order.

b His direct address to the reader makes his opinion of war very clear. He implies that if readers are 'decent human beings' they will share his opinion. Students should recognise that readers are being manipulated here.

c Students should explore the implications of 'They get the bill' – the ways in which the poor are made to pay for war. They may also investigate implicit bias against the rich in the preceding sentence.

d There is an opportunity here for students to explore the range of feelings McCullin reveals. Students could comment on his sense of duty, his compulsion to reveal the truth and to communicate it to others. They should also be encouraged to explore his references to guilt and the reasons why he may feel guilty.

Chapter 9
Alternative interpretations

e The final sentence suggests he abhors war and all it entails. Students should be able to point out the irony that war can have a positive aspect in the compassion it can sometimes bring out in people.

Exploring alternative interpretations

It is important to stress to students that considering alternative interpretations is a higher-order skill which they will need to demonstrate in exams and controlled assessment to gain the highest grades.

Activity 2 As there will be a focus on listening to and challenging of the opinions of others in this activity, there are opportunities for the teaching and/or assessment of oral skills as a Discussing and listening activity. Group or paired discussion leading to whole-class feedback would expose students to a range of interpretations, thus reinforcing the idea that everyone's interpretation is valid as long as it is rooted in the text.

Activity 3 This allows students to reflect on the ideas they have formulated so far and to develop their interpretations in more detail. Students could show their work to another student for peer assessment. The peer assessor should check whether their partner has given alternative interpretations of the areas covered by the bullet points in the Student Book, offering suggestions for developing ideas if needed. The best responses could be used for a whole-class display, with annotations indicating where alternative interpretations have been developed.

Analysing the writer's perspective and use of language

k! Analysis activity: Understanding the cultural context of a text

Before tackling the second text you could ask students what they already know of the work of George Orwell. Some research, either as a homework or a class activity, could prepare students for the extract from *The Road to Wigan Pier*.

In order to assist students in their understanding of a writer's perspective, they could be asked to write a few lines of description of a view of a street from the perspective of a person who enjoyed living there or from the perspective of someone who hated living there. Both descriptions should cover the same details, for example, houses, trees, traffic, children playing.

A comparison of favourable and unfavourable descriptions should reinforce understanding of how a writer's feelings can affect the way she/he writes about a place.

Activity 4 (Worksheet 9b) It should be stressed that considering the impact of individual words and phrases is an important part of interpreting a text. An alternative approach to this task could be to give students a list of the words and phrases from the table in the Student Book and ask them to explain what they think is suggested by each. The examples could be broken down in this way:

- 'a mixture of cinders and frozen mud'
- 'crisscrossed by the imprints of innumerable clogs'
- 'a dreadful afternoon'
- 'It was horribly cold.'

Students could also be asked to highlight what they feel is the key word in each example.

If the table activity is used, here are some possible responses:

Example	Impact on reader
The canal path was a mixture of cinders and frozen mud, crisscrossed by the imprint of innumerable clogs …	Portrays an unattractive image of the place. 'Imprint of innumerable clogs' suggests many unpleasant journeys have been made along the canal.
I remember a dreadful afternoon in the environs of Wigan.	'Dreadful' portrays a very negative opinion, suggesting it was so horrible as to be imprinted on his memory. It arouses the curiosity of the reader, who might wonder what was so awful about Wigan.
It was horribly cold.	Makes the reader share his discomfort. Students may link the word 'horribly' with 'dreadful' to comment on their combined effect. It seems to sum up the atmosphere of the whole place.

Activity 5

Key features of Text C are:

- the structure of the response begins with a summary of the writer's feelings
- the vocabulary used to introduce interpretation
- the development of the student's own ideas about the writer's perspective
- the detailed comments on the effects of individual words and phrases.

Students should incorporate these features into their own response. You may wish to use peer assessment to check that all the features are present. A peer assessor could annotate a partner's text in the same way that the sample text in the Student Book has been annotated.

Reviewing your learning

k! Planning activity: The writer's viewpoint

Activity 6 You may wish to allow students to complete the tasks in Activities 6 and 7 without preparation in order to assess their ability to work independently. Suggested responses are as follows:

a   She was in a confident mood and felt she was not in danger.

b   The colour of the rhino reveals to readers just how close she was to the animals; it draws them into the account.

c   The line beginning 'that little pale eye' makes the reader aware of the danger she was in. The fact that this is the last sentence in the paragraph creates tension and compels the reader to continue.

d   Students should note that the second person is used in the third paragraph, when the danger is most imminent. It adds a note of immediacy to the account and helps the reader to appreciate the writer's perspective.

e   The first simile, 'a flat boulder that raised him like a pedestal', makes the rhino appear important and dominant – even menacing. In the second simile, the use of the word 'monument' continues the effect created by the word 'pedestal'. It makes him appear majestic and terrifying at the same time.

Activity 7 This activity allows students the opportunity to practise the skills they have used so far in this chapter. You may wish to ask them to assess their progress by commenting on how much they feel they have achieved, using the bullet points as a checklist.

Stretch yourself

Students could use their school library as a source of travel writing or they could be directed to look in local bookshops. Although it is not practical to ask them to buy books, they could report back on their findings from browsing.

In order to enable students to focus more closely on a text, you could provide them with a choice of extracts from the work of Bill Bryson (for example, *Notes from a Small Island* or *A Walk in the Woods*).

Outcomes

In this chapter your students have:

- read texts closely
- formed their own ideas about meanings in texts
- developed an understanding of writers' perspectives
- made a detailed analysis of language and its impact on the reader.

10 Making comparisons

AO focus

English AO2 Reading and English Language AO3 Studying written language.

- Read and understand texts, selecting material appropriate to purpose, collating from different sources and making comparisons and cross references as appropriate.
- Explain and evaluate how writers use linguistic, grammatical, structural and presentational features to achieve effects and engage and influence the reader.

In this chapter your students will:

- study two texts, thinking about and making notes on audience and purpose, use of presentational features, and use of language
- study the features of a written comparison and write their own comparison.

Additional resources

Worksheets

10a: Comparing purpose and audience
10b: Comparing presentational features

Getting started

This chapter draws together much of the learning in the Reading section of the Student Book. You might like to put key terms on the board and ask students to identify their meaning from memory prior to starting the chapter. The key terms could include:

- purpose
- audience
- presentational features
- images
- font styles
- evaluate
- emotive language
- rhetorical questions.

Working through the chapter

Purpose and audience

Students have already done a lot of work on purpose and audience. This is an opportunity to check that they have genuinely grasped the meanings and implications of these features.

Activity 1 (Worksheet 10a) The completed tables below and on page 40 show the kinds of things students might put in their tables. Where possible, encourage students to share ideas in pairs or small groups, and to highlight common features in purpose and audience. All identified purpose(s) and audience(s) should be matched by a 'reason for thinking this' and purposes or audiences common to both texts should be highlighted.

Text A	Reasons for thinking this	Text B	Reasons for thinking this
Purpose(s)		Purpose(s)	
• To raise awareness.	Uses true stories to show what happens to people when human rights are not respected.	• To inform.	Facts, e.g. 'many still live in ruined buildings with no electricity or mains water supply.'
• To make people angry about the injustice.	Invites people to place themselves in the situation of the victims of injustice to understand what it must feel like.	• To raise awareness.	Give details of the work of MSF's volunteers.
• To persuade people to support Amnesty.	The use of rhetorical questions and the Amnesty address.	• To make the reader want to support MSF.	Includes a true story of one man's fight against TB.

English and English Language Teacher's Book Higher Tier
Section A: Reading

Text A	Reasons for thinking this	Text B	Reasons for thinking this
Audience(s)		Audience(s)	
• People interested in the work of Amnesty.	It's part of a leaflet that people would pick up and read if they were interested in finding out more.	• Current supporters of MSF.	It would probably be current supporters who would be reading the magazine.
• People who care about freedom and human rights.	It appeals to the reader's ideas of fairness and justice and shows what happens where these do not apply.	• People who might be thinking of volunteering for MSF.	Provides the details and personal account of one such volunteer.
• People who might become supporters of Amnesty.	Appeals directly to the reader with the use of the second-person pronoun 'you' and asks questions to involve the reader and gain support, e.g. 'And what could be more important to protect?'		

Presentational features

Analysis activity: Comparing teen magazine websites

It is worth reiterating the message that identification of features is a relatively low-level skill. It is the comment on the feature that demonstrates the understanding of the reader and the quality of that comment that demonstrates the level of understanding.

Activity 2 (Worksheet 10b) Students are likely to identify a wide range of presentational features. For Text A these may include:

- use of colour: vibrant pink, black
- font sizes and use of bold
- barbed-wire image
- central written text 'framed' by colour/images at sides
- Amnesty symbol: candle and barbed wire.

For Text B these may include:

- headline: use of bold
- photographs
- map
- use of colour.

When completing their comments in the second column, students should consider what they discovered in Activity 1 about purpose and audience. In giving their opinion on effectiveness they are evaluating the feature or making a judgement on it. You might want to refer students back to the work done on evaluation in Chapter 4.

Encourage students to discuss their findings. You might want to cover this in class rather than group discussion, to ensure comments on effectiveness are supported by considered opinion. Remind students at the end of the activity to place an asterisk beside any presentational features that are common to both texts.

Developing your comments

Students often find it difficult to put their ideas into writing. The annotated extract from a student's answer shows them how the developed comment has been constructed. They need to learn how to do this in order to achieve highly in their controlled assessments and their exam. You might want to give students copies of Text C to annotate and keep for revision purposes.

Activity 3 This provides students with the opportunity to practise what they have learned. Students should use the prompts to help them think about the image before writing their answers. You may wish to collate their ideas in response to (a) on the board before asking them to write their answers. This would allow them to concentrate on the writing skills they need to develop here.

Developing comments on language

Analysis activity: Comparing motorcycle safety websites

This section provides prompts for features that students can identify in the texts. You may want to run through this list to check their understanding of each feature before they start the next activity.

Activity 4 Here are some examples of features students may identify. There are others. Remind them to note examples of the features they identify.

Text A:

- **Language:** the language is relatively simple, though contains some complex terms (for example, 'highly repressive regime', 'lofty concept').

Chapter 10
Making comparisons

- **Rhetorical questions:** for example, 'What could possibly be of greater value than that?'
- **Repetition:** for example, 'where there are no human rights, there is no safety, no protection, no shelter, no hope and – all too often – no life'.
- **Tenses:** there is a shift from the past when imagining (for example, 'you were') to the present when presenting facts (for example, 'what is true for them, is true for us all').

Text B:

- **Sentence structures:** these are generally complex. (For example, 'TB is a massive problem here, but there are only five functioning TB clinics in the whole of Chechnya, serving one million people.')
- **Adjectives:** for example, '**incredibly rare**', '**deadly** problem', '**major** setback'.
- **Pronouns:** for example, 'like **me**', 'from **our**'.
- **Emotive language:** for example, 'deadly problem', 'continue the long battle'.

The extract from a student's answer (Text D) demonstrates how to develop ideas on linguistic features in writing, something that many students find difficult to do. The student takes one word, 'imagine', and explores its meaning and analyses its use in the text as a whole. Spend some time with students analysing the content and construction of the comment. You might want to do this on the whiteboard, adding the given annotations as you work through.

It is important that students realise that they do not have to write about every language feature in order to do well. They do, however, have to demonstrate the skill of analysis. Again, an annotated copy of Text D would be a useful revision prompt for each student to keep.

Activity 5 This directs students to think more carefully about specific features of language use and to make notes on the different things that could be put in a written answer. Encourage them to share ideas, both in pairs and in small groups. Alternatively, this could be done as a class exercise, with you collating ideas on the board.

Activity 6 Students now take one feature to write about in detail. Encourage them to reread the student answer given earlier before they write their developed comment. Remind them that their aim is to demonstrate the ability to analyse language. Once complete, you could ask them to annotate their answer using the annotated Text D as a model.

Writing a comparison

Planning activity: Making comparisons

This section takes students through how to write a comparison of two texts. It is important for them to note that superficial comparisons – for example, colour is used in both texts – are of little value; they would need to explore and compare how colour is used in each text. As before, aim to help reinforce the need to focus on a few significant features: students who try to cover everything in an exam rarely succeed in demonstrating analysis.

Students are first shown how to analyse a question, to ensure they answer in an appropriate and focused way. They are also given an example of a plan that notes key points only. Remind students that plans do not need to be detailed, but they do need to be focused.

They should study the writing and the annotations closely to help them identify the high-level skills. This could be done as a class activity, matching annotations to text on the whiteboard. Once these elements of the answer have been identified, you should spend time considering the language of comparison as indicated by the highlighted words. You could collate and list these on the board and add other useful words and phrases to the list such as: 'however', 'similarly', 'in comparison', 'different in that', 'like', 'different from'.

Activity 7 This activity requires students to use what they have learned about writing a comparison. It may help to set a time limit of 30 minutes for this activity. You could also ask students to swap responses and highlight indicators of exploration, analysis, evaluation and comparison. Alternatively, you may wish to assess their responses in this light and set targets accordingly.

Stretch yourself

This puts the students in the position of 'expert', where they have to use their knowledge to guide others. You could define the audience more precisely (for example, students of your own age, students in Y9). Encourage students to read through the chapter before writing their guide, and, where desirable, allow them to work in pairs. Make clear that they can use subheadings, bullet points and other presentational features to enhance their guide. Provide the opportunity for them to compare their guides and comment on any significant omissions in them.

Outcomes

In this chapter your students have:

- considered the purposes and audiences of two texts
- explored uses of presentational features in two texts
- examined the uses of language in two texts
- compared the uses of presentation and language features for effect in two texts.

11 Making your reading skills count in the exam

AO focus

English AO2 Reading and English Language AO3 Studying written language.

- Read and understand texts, selecting material appropriate to purpose, collating from different sources and making comparisons and cross-references as appropriate.
- Explain and evaluate how writers use linguistic, grammatical, structural and presentational features to achieve effects and engage and influence the reader.

In this chapter your students will:

- learn more about how their reading is tested in the exam
- study texts and questions in a sample paper
- consider how to achieve high marks in their answers.

Additional resources

Worksheets

11a: Analysing sample answers to Question 1
11b: Analysing sample answers to Question 4

Working through the chapter

About the exam

This section makes clear what students have to do in their GCSE English or GCSE English Language exam. It is worth stressing the significant number of marks that students can gain by doing well in this.

What you need to know

The Assessment Objectives are written for teachers, not students. This section of the Student Book breaks down the Assessment Objectives and explains them in ways that have meaning for the students. It is important that students are helped to internalise these; to do this, they need to be helped to access the language. You may want to do a quick check on their understanding of the terminology. You could ask them to pair up the term and the appropriate explanation of it from the items below. The terms from the Assessment Objectives are highlighted:

> understanding   techniques, methods
> textual reference   appropriate to purpose
> evaluate   inference, deduction, exploration
> and interpretation   make judgements on

> collate   quote from or refer to details in the text   how writers use   have an effect on   use material from two different texts to answer question   make comparison
> the words used   linguistic techniques
> point out similarities and differences   influence

Students should be made aware that all these skills have been covered in the Reading chapters in the Student Book.

Sample questions

k! Write and assess activity: The Reading exam 1
k! Write and assess activity: The Reading exam 2

The questions in the exam are based on the Assessment Objectives. The bullet points after each question in the Student Book show the link between the question and the Assessment Objectives. As an alternative approach to simply reading the questions and the related AOs, you could put the questions on the board and ask students to work out exactly what is being assessed in each question. The more accomplished students are at doing this, the better they are able to give focused answers in the exam.

When reading the questions, students should also be encouraged to take note of the marks awarded to each one. It is particularly important that they note that Question 4, the comparison question, carries twice the number of marks of Questions 1 to 3. They only have 1 hour for reading and need to balance their time carefully. As a simple guide, they could allow 10 minutes for reading the questions and texts, 10 minutes for each of Questions 1 to 3, and 20 minutes for Question 4.

Activity 1 Having read the questions, students are directed to read the texts and make notes on the answers to each question. They could work in pairs or small groups. You should allow 20–30 minutes for them to do this. You could collate their notes before moving on to the next section on sample answers.

Sample answers

This section is designed to help students write focused answers that will gain high marks. Students often learn best through the analysis of other students' responses rather than their own. Having considered potential answers to the questions, they are in a position to better judge the quality of the sample responses.

Activity 2 (Worksheet 11a) Students are asked to identify the skills demonstrated in two sample responses to Question 1. You could ask them to identify what the student is doing in each sentence. The tables below offer a possible analysis of the two responses. Note that the responses are of similar length. Students often believe that longer responses are better and often spend too long on their answers to the first two questions. It is important that they realise that it is the quality of the response and not its length that gains the marks.

Encourage students to articulate in their own words what Student A needs to do to achieve a higher mark. In collation of their ideas you might emphasise the need to adopt an overview and to make perceptive comments.

Text D:

Skill demonstrated	Example from student's writing
Offers relevant quotation/a little interpretation	The writer seems to be quite excited about the exhibition at first because she talks about it being 'momentous'.
Understands meaning/offers relevant and appropriate quotation	She also says it is 'near-legendary' which means that these warriors have been around for a long time.
Understands meaning	But then, even though she says people should definitely go and see it, she points out all the things that are wrong with it like there are only 20 figures and some bits of them are missing like the archer's bow.
Considers impact on the reader	That might make people less likely to go but if they read on they will still want to because she seems to say that it doesn't matter that it's not a full army.
Offers relevant quotation	She thinks the exhibition designers have done a brilliant job because you get to see the figures as real people: 'people that we recognise and know'.
Offers relevant quotation	At the end of the article she says these figures will keep you 'spellbound'
Interprets information	as though you'll never want to stop looking at them
Develops comment	and that the exhibition is really about them and not the Emperor at all even though it talks about the Emperor in the headline.

Text E:

Skill demonstrated	Example from student's writing
Adopts an overview/makes perceptive comment	The writer moves from excitement, through scepticism to arrive finally at enchantment.
Offers relevant quotation/ considers the impact on the reader/adopts an overview	She offers a fair and honest analysis for the reader acknowledging the potential hazards of 'the crush', the initial disappointments of the 'rather shabby' figures, but then capturing our imagination with her account of how it feels to 'stand and stare' at each individual figure.
Engages with the text as an article	This is not about an army, or even a platoon, as the article's sub-heading suggests.
Makes perceptive comment	This is about the individual – the person behind the figure, both its creator and its model.
Interprets information	In these figures she perceives the range of ethnic origins and, more significantly, the individual characters – the characters we meet in our everyday modern lives, the characters to whom we are directly related.
Offers relevant quotation	It is this 'sense of relation' that causes her ultimately to so strongly recommend the exhibition and to refer to its designers as having 'succeeded so brilliantly'.
Offers relevant quotation/ evidence of understanding/ considers impact on reader	The temptation to stand 'spellbound' in front of these figures would be difficult for any reader to resist.

English and English Language Teacher's Book Higher Tier
Section A: Reading

Activity 3 Students are shown a response to Question 2, with the features of the response highlighted. It is worth mentioning that many students spend too much time describing what they see and fail to analyse and comment perceptively.

Encourage students to discuss the colours and images before suggesting additional points. Here are two examples of how points could have been developed.

- The picture of the three 'Vikings' is placed directly beneath the text, which encourages the reader to find out more about Vikings. All three are looking straight at the reader, as though challenging or threatening them. Although their expressions are threatening, they are not particularly frightening, so do not disturb the relatively calm and happy mood created by the other two images. Perhaps, as children are clearly an intended audience, the intention was to make them look exciting and fun rather than genuinely scary.

- There is a contrast in the use of colour between the two sections. The orange of the first suggests light glowing, as though suggesting light will be thrown on the past through a visit to Jorvik. The block of orange, against which the text is set, is shadowed to suggest a curtain. It's as though the curtain is hiding the mysteries of the past and the reader needs to draw it aside to explore the darker reality of Viking times, as echoed in the dark background of the second section. Once the curtain is drawn, 'You are in JORVIK!', as the text tells you.

You could collate additional points made by students. When doing so, it is important not to discount any suggestions made by students, as this can dampen confidence and affect their willingness to make their own judgements in the future. Having collated the points, however, you could ask students to decide which of these demonstrate the highest level of reading skills and explore the reasons for their choices.

Activity 4

Progress tracking: The Reading exam 3

The suggestions contained in (a) to (c) show students the kind of things they need to write about in order to answer Question 3 well. The intention is not that they should write a full answer, but that they should develop comments that could be included in an answer. You may wish to use the comments above as examples of developed comment. Students could initially work in pairs and then share their prepared comments with another pair, selecting the best of both.

An example of a possible response is given below:

a The boy presents a mixture of impressions of both the beach and the 'wall of water' which almost prevents him from finding his 'treasure'. Though clearly aware of the danger it poses, he will not give up his search and is almost reckless in his determination. His 'greed for treasure' is evident as he pursues his search despite 'another great wave' gathering behind him.

b The boy believes he can find the 'treasure' that he associates with the 'journey of life' and is determined to do so. He is not disheartened by the size of the task ahead of him nor by the wave that threatens to overcome him. Despite danger, he retains his hope that the 'crescent of green and silver' will again appear and is finally rewarded for his perseverance.

Initially the boy seems to feel no fear, bending to pick up the copper wire and ignoring the sea crashing to his right. He seems afraid when the wave knocks him over and certainly realises the danger as being, potentially, 'the beginning of a vast silence'. However, despite this brush with death, he continues and ignores the next 'great wave' to find his treasure. His fear is short-lived and completely overcome by his need to find the 'treasure'.

c At times the writer has an adult voice, as in the opening sentence, where he generalises and philosophises. At other times we see things through the child's eyes. The beach is compared to 'the pink skin beneath the fur of an animal', which seems a childlike image. The shred of old copper wire is kept because it is 'of some value to the treasure hunter', again a childlike action and thought. Furthermore there is no adult caution evident when the boy continues to search, despite the power of the waves and awareness of the danger.

Activity 5 (Worksheet 11b) Students are invited to compare two extracts from responses to Question 4 and to identify why Student B's comments are worth more marks than those of Student A. They could work in pairs or small groups. They are likely to identify that Student B:

- selects details from across the text
- analyses the use of language
- comments perceptively
- links language use with purpose
- makes comparative points
- makes detailed textual references.

Students are then asked to write their own complete answer to Question 4. They should aim

44

to focus on other aspects of language use in both texts. Once they have completed their answer it would be helpful for them to annotate it using the bullet points given to them in part (b).

Encourage students to exchange and assess responses by identifying what is done well.

Students are often unwilling to learn from the mistakes they have made in exams. However, when placed in the position of 'expert' and 'assessor', they are able to utilise their knowledge and learn the necessary lessons from the mistakes made by others. The approaches in this chapter can be adapted and used for any exam for Reading. It is worth noting also that students often benefit most from short exam practice sessions. Asking them to do the answer to one question and then to consider and assess possible responses can be more productive than simply getting them to do a full practice paper. This is a particularly helpful approach if linked directly to the study of a specific area, such as use of linguistic devices.

Outcomes

In this chapter your students have:

- studied how the Assessment Objective for Reading is tested in the exam
- examined texts and questions in a sample paper
- considered how to achieve the highest marks they can in their exam.

12 Making your reading skills count in the controlled assessment

AO focus

English AO2 Reading and English Language AO3 Studying written language.

- Read and understand texts, selecting material appropriate to purpose, collating from different sources and making comparisons and cross-references as appropriate.
- Develop and sustain interpretations of writers' ideas and perspectives.
- Explain and evaluate how writers use linguistic, grammatical, structural and presentational features to achieve effects and engage and influence the reader.
- [English AO2 only] Understand texts in their social, cultural and historical contexts.

In this chapter your students will:

- learn more about how their reading skills are tested in the controlled assessment
- explore the different choices available to them
- consider how to achieve high marks in their controlled assessment.

Additional resources

Worksheets

12a: Answering a question on Themes and ideas
12b: Analysing a student's response

Working through the chapter

The reading requirements are different in the two specifications.

GCSE English

Students need to respond to:

- a play by Shakespeare
- a prose text from either a different culture or the English Literary Heritage
- a poetry text from either a different culture or the English Literary Heritage

Students will explore each of these texts by responding to the same task. For example, the task may invite students to explore the characterisation of the central character of the text, or to explore a theme like family relationships. The same task will apply to each text.

GCSE English Language

Students need to respond to one 'extended text'. A text consists of:

- a novel
- a collection of 7 short stories
- a play
- a collection of 15 poems
- a literary non-fiction text (e.g. biography or travel writing).

Students will have a choice of tasks from which they choose one. In this specification students will have up to 4 hours of controlled assessment time to be spent on one text, whereas in GCSE English the same amount of time is devoted to three texts, suggesting that in GCSE English Language the response will be more wide-ranging in the way a single text is explored.

What is controlled assessment?

You may have a class of students who are all taking the same specification, which will make it relatively straightforward to explain the single set of requirements. If you are dealing with a situation in which you have students who are being entered for different specifications, or who might in the future be entered for different specifications, then it would be sensible to focus on the similarities, the common features:

- basically the same AOs
- the same amount of time
- similar tasks
- the same ground rules for preparation and then undertaking the controlled assessment.

GCSE English

There is one Assessment Objective that applies only to GCSE English: 'understand texts in their social, cultural and historical contexts.' There is no requirement for this AO to be applied to all three texts in the controlled assessment, but it must feature somewhere.

> The best way to approach these contexts is to begin with the text being studied. If, for example, the English Literary Heritage text being studied is *Oliver Twist*, the most sensible way to find out how society and culture were different in Dickens' time is to explore the novel. Students will achieve nothing by including potted biographies of Charles Dickens or hugely generalised information about life in Victorian England. By generalising, about the position of women in society, for example, students present a very stereotypical, bland view of an era they may know little about.
>
> The key point about the contexts is that any response to them needs to be relevant to the task in hand. If, for example, the task was to explore 'family relationships' in a text like *Romeo and Juliet*, it would be best to begin with the family relationships in the play. Exploring the relationship between Capulet and Juliet would lead most students to the realisation that social values have changed over the centuries. Far better to respond to this than to introduce some ideas about Elizabethan values which are likely to be overgeneralised.
>
> The same approach would be necessary in the response to a text from a different culture. The best way to find out about American culture and society in the 1930s as it applies to *Of Mice and Men* is to explore the text. That might lead to some light historical research, but any observations must be rooted in the text.

The ground rules about the actual controlled assessment task are quite straightforward, but those concerning the planning, preparatory stage need to be clearly explained:

- 'Notes' must not constitute a pre-prepared draft.
- Students must keep a scrupulous record of any resources they use to help them prepare.
- The teacher is not allowed to comment on a prepared draft and give feedback before the controlled assessment.

It is worthwhile drawing the attention of students to the advice about selecting important parts of a text for analysis. Notes should include some form of list of the sections of text that are going to form the basis of the student's response.

Introducing the tasks

On your marks activity: The Reading controlled assessment 1

Higher-tier students should be familiar with the ideas of theme and characterisation.

Themes and ideas

It would be a good idea to identify a literary text that the group is studying and to invite responses to a question about what the main themes or ideas are.

It would be a good idea to have student-friendly versions of the AOs on display for constant reference.

Some words from the AOs are of particular significance for higher-tier students: 'develop and sustain'. Students will probably understand the words, but will need to fully grasp their significance. One effect of the National Strategy has been to spread use of the PEE (point, evidence, explain) formula, which leads to quite simple writing in the middle and lower grades. Higher-tier students will need to grasp the importance of a word like 'develop'. This should be reflected in notes: a 'point' will need subsequent strands. Mind-mapping enthusiasts could well display how mind-mapping techniques may help students extend a point of understanding.

Characterisation and voice

This is largely straightforward, but it might be a good idea to draw attention to the difference between character and characterisation. The focus should be on characterisation – that is, the ways in which a character is created, developed and used by a writer. The key part of the AO is:

- Explain and evaluate how writers use linguistic, grammatical, structural and presentational features to achieve effects and engage and influence the reader.

The emphasis here is clearly on the **techniques** used by writers to 'achieve effects and engage and influence the reader.' Writing about characters as though they are real people is something that students slip into very easily and they need to be shown the correct focus at an early stage.

Sample tasks and sample answers

You may only have to focus on one of the specification panels in the Student Book. If you do have to address both though, the panels should make it fairly straightforward to see a great deal of common ground.

The information in these panels should lead to some discussion of time management. There are significant differences between the two specifications: in one, students have to write about three texts and in the other it is only one text, but the same amount of time is allocated. It is very important in the case of GCSE English that students realise they have about an hour to

English and English Language Teacher's Book Higher Tier
Section A: Reading

write about a text, and that as they prepare their notes they have the limitations of time firmly in their sights.

Because there is choice of texts, it is impossible to provide activities in the Student Book covering the three areas required for English – drama, prose and poetry, covering Shakespeare, ELH, different cultures. The example given is based on poetry from the ELH and focuses on a potential theme. Work undertaken by students would also be of use to those studying GCSE English Literature.

Activity 1

k! Connecting comments activity: The Reading controlled assessment 2

k! Planning activity: The Reading controlled assessment 3

The two poems in this activity are taken from the *AQA Anthology*. Annotated copies of texts may not be taken into the controlled assessment, but working on the annotation of a clean text has obvious benefits at the preparation and planning stage.

a Before students move on to 'Storm in the Black Forest', it would be a good idea to invite small groups to discuss any additions they might make to the annotations on 'Below the Green Corrie'. The annotations focus on the key element of the task – people's relationship with nature – and on 'the ways', the techniques used by the writer.

b (Worksheet 12a) Some suggested annotations are shown in the table at the bottom of this page.

The timings in the plan are very rough guidelines, but given the timing restrictions of controlled assessment, it would be worthwhile discussing timings and planning for them in the preparation stage.

Activity 2
It would be helpful to elicit students' responses to the two passages before they read the teacher's comments. They will all identify the best response, but it would be helpful to tease out explicitly the elements of the second response which make it better – mainly the way ideas are 'sustained and developed'. One way of showing this would be to look at what is written about 'bandits' in each response.

Highlighted phrase	Annotation
bronzey soft sky	Suggests the writer sees beauty in nature – the repetition of the 's' sounds opens the poem in a gentle tone.
jugfull after jugfull of pure white liquid fire, bright white	Describing the sheet lightning as liquid, using the commonplace 'jugfull', removes any sense of fear; it is an unusual but quite gentle image.
gold-bronze flutters	The colours again suggest beauty and the word 'flutters' is a soft, gentle word.
sometimes/a still brighter white snake wriggles among it, spilled/ and tumbling wriggling down the sky	The introduction of 'snake' to describe the forked lightning introduces a potentially more menacing tone, but that is balanced by the almost playful sense of the repeated 'wriggles', 'wriggling'.
the heavens cackle with uncouth sounds	There is a suggestion of the supernatural here, as 'cackle' suggests witchcraft. 'Uncouth' suggests wildness, lack of civility.
electricity	Introduces an element of science – a shift in the poem from a romantic portrayal of the power of nature to a scientific interpretation of what lightning is.
is supposed to have mastered/ chained, subjugated to his use!	The use of three variations on the idea of enslaving, alongside the repeated 'supposed to' reveals the writer's main idea, which seems to concern the beautiful power of nature being beyond the control of man and science.

Activity 3 (Worksheet 12b) Examples of possible advice students could give are included in the table below.

Text E	Possible advice
The writer is describing a storm in the Black Forest one evening, 'Now it is almost night'.	The choice of quotation is not very good – it does not support the previous statement.
In the first five lines he describes the lightning as though someone is pouring it down from the sky, 'Jugfull'. He points out how very white the lightning is because he repeats the word.	Both observations are 'correct', but neither relates to the task; there is nothing about how these two images show the writer's relationship with nature. The reference to 'white' is not related to the other use of colour in the poem.
In the middle of the poem he changes from describing the lightning as being a liquid. Instead he calls it a 'snake'. This shows that his feelings for nature aren't very good because snakes aren't very nice.	This is better: there is an attempt to comment on the writer's choice of words and to relate it to the idea of people's relationship with nature, but the comment 'aren't very nice' could easily have been developed.
He also mentions the thunder and makes it sound like a witch, 'the heavens cackle with uncouth sounds'.	This reverts to the fairly weak approach in the first paragraph where something is noticed, but only mentioned rather than explored.
In the end he shows that people think they are wonderful, that they can control anything, but in reality they can't control things like the power of lightning because he says 'man is supposed to have mastered' electricity, the phrase 'supposed to' shows that the writer thinks man hasn't been able to control nature, nature is still all powerful.	This is certainly focused on the key element of the task and reveals understanding of the central idea of the poem, but the student misses an opportunity to explore the effect of the repetition in the final lines, and misses the impact of the exclamation marks. There is no attempt to relate this final section of the poem to what has preceded it, so the references to structure – 'In the end' – are not convincing.

Outcomes

In this chapter your students have:

- learned about how their reading skills are tested in the controlled assessment
- learned more about the ways they can achieve high marks in this part of the course.

Section B: Writing

Overview

Section B of the Student Book is designed to develop students' skills in writing as defined by the Assessment Objectives for GCSE English (AO3 Writing) and GCSE English Language (AO4 Writing) and tested in the exam and the controlled assessments.

GCSE English: AO3 Writing
GCSE English Language: AO4 Writing

- Write [to communicate] clearly, effectively and imaginatively, using and adapting forms and selecting vocabulary appropriate to task and purpose in ways that engage the reader.
- Organise information and ideas into structured and sequenced sentences, paragraphs and whole texts, using a variety of linguistic and structural features to support cohesion and overall coherence.
- Use a range of sentence structures for clarity, purpose and effect, with accurate punctuation and spelling.

The chapters provide opportunities for students to draw on and revise the skills they have already acquired in writing, and to develop these further. The learning objectives, founded in the Assessment Objectives but in 'student-friendly' language, are given at the start of each chapter. Throughout each chapter the learning points are clarified and modelled, and followed by activities that are designed to reinforce and extend students' learning.

Students are encouraged to work independently or in pairs or small groups, as appropriate, and are given regular opportunities to assess their personal progress and that of other students, often against fixed criteria. The learning within the chapters is cumulative, building on what has come before, and at the end of several chapters there is a summative activity that challenges students to demonstrate their learning across the whole section.

Each chapter can be used as a discrete stand-alone topic, with activities and tasks specific to the named objectives. The order in which they appear in the Student Book does not have to be followed, though it is worth noting that this order was arrived at after careful consideration of how best to build students' skills in writing.

Assessment

GCSE English	*GCSE English Language*
External examination: Writing non-fiction texts (1 hour)	**External examination:** Writing non-fiction texts (1 hour)
Controlled assessment: Producing creative texts (up to 4 hours)	**Controlled assessment:** Creative writing (up to 4 hours)

Section B
Writing

Nelson Thornes resources

Chapter	Student Book activities	kerboodle! resources
13: Getting your message across	1–2: Identifying methods of communication and considering purpose and audience 3: Listing and prioritising important features of clear communication 4: Writing complete sentences 5: Matching subjects and verbs 6: Using the correct tense 7: Practising using commas 8: Using a range of punctuation in a piece of extended writing 9–10: Rewriting to avoid ambiguity 11: Writing to advise other students on how to communicate clearly	• Text transformer activity: Writing clearly 1 • Learning activity: Subject–verb agreement • Learning activity: Matching tenses • Text transformer activity: Writing clearly 2 • Worksheet 13a: Making your meaning clear
14: Making the right choices	1: Writing a text message poem 2: Evaluating when it is and is not appropriate to use text message language 3–5: Using formal and informal language in emails 6–7: Using appropriate language in letters to suit purpose and audience 8: Rewriting text for a different purpose 9: Writing a letter to express an opinion	• Analysis activity: Comparing formality • Learning activity: Formal and informal writing • Learning activity: Using language for different audiences and purposes • Analysis activity: Form, audience and purpose • Worksheet 14a: Text messages
15: Organising writing	1: Ordering sentences 2: Continuing a piece of writing, developing points 3: Analysing the order of sentences in a paragraph 4–5: Linking ideas within a paragraph 6: Analysing how descriptive writing is organised 7: Planning and writing a descriptive paragraph 8–9: Analysing and writing a story opening	• Learning activity: Organising information • Learning activity: Organised writing • Write and assess activity: Writing cohesively • Analysis activity: How texts hang together • Worksheet 15a: Sequencing sentences • Worksheet 15b: Organising sentences into paragraphs
16: Getting the words right	1: Writing using the same vowel in every word 2–3: Choosing and using synonyms 4: Writing a description and varying the tone 5–7: Identifying vocabulary choices and descriptive techniques in a text 8: Explaining how metaphors are used in a text 9–11: Organising descriptions into paragraphs	• Learning activity: Choosing vocabulary 1 • Learning activity: Choosing vocabulary 2 • Analysis activity: Word choices 1 • Text transformer activity: Word choices 2 • Worksheet 16a: Writing techniques 1 • Worksheet 16b: Writing techniques 2

English and English Language Teacher's Book Higher Tier
Section B: Writing

Chapter	Student Book activities	kerboodle! resources
17: Making sense of sentences	1: Matching sentence types to audience and purpose 2: Identifying how writers choose sentence structures for their audience and purpose 3: Rewriting sentences for a different audience 4: Writing using a range of sentence structures to create variety and emphasis 5: Identifying sentence patterns and their uses 6: Writing a paragraph using sentence patterns 7–8: Analysing and using sentences to create effects 9: Using commas to create effects Stretch yourself: Writing to advise, using appropriate sentence structures	• Learning activity: Sentence structures • Learning activity: Sentence effects • Analysis activity: Sentence patterns • Connecting comments activity: Using a range of sentences in writing • Text transformer activity: Combining sentences • Worksheet 17a: Creating patterns: lists and repetitions
18: Getting it together 1: non-fiction writing	1: Self-evaluating planning methods 2–5: Identifying organisational features in news articles 6: Organising ideas to write a news article 7: Putting a news article in the correct order 8: Structuring writing to express a view 9: Commenting on how complex sentences are linked together 10–11: Planning and writing a newspaper article	• Planning activity: Argumentative writing • Planning activity: Informative writing • Worksheet 18a: Planning your writing • Worksheet 18b: Structuring your writing
19: Getting it together 2: fiction writing	1: Writing a mini-saga 2–4: Analysing and writing paragraphs organised chronologically 5–6: Analysing and writing paragraphs using flashbacks 7–8: Analysing and writing paragraphs using a twist Stretch yourself: Analysing and writing poetry	• Learning activity: Mini-saga • Learning activity: Writing descriptively • Write and assess activity: Organising events in a story • Connecting comments activity: Assessing creative writing • Worksheet 19a: Planning a story based on a photograph
20: Meeting the needs of your readers	1: Identifying purpose 2: Analysing and using techniques to engage the reader 3: Identifying techniques used by writers to maintain readers' interest 4: Writing a review using techniques to maintain readers' interest 5: Analysing how writers influence their readers 6: Writing an article to entertain readers 7: Analysing how writers use detail to interest their readers 8: Writing a descriptive paragraph Stretch yourself: Analysing how a writer structures a text and builds up detail; writing a description using details to interest the readers	• Learning activity: Vocabulary and audience • Learning activity: Influencing your readers • Analysis activity: Tourism texts • Connecting comments activity: Detail and description • Worksheet 20a: Thinking about purpose • Worksheet 20b: Influencing your readers • Worksheet 20c: Adding details to interest your readers 1 • Worksheet 20d: Adding details to interest your readers 2

Section B
Writing

Chapter	Student Book activities	kerboodle! resources
21: Different kinds of writing	1–4: Identifying genres and identifying some of their characteristics 5: Rewriting an extract to fit another genre 6: Analysing features of two genres 7: Writing in two different genres 8–9: Analysing how one genre can be transformed into another: prose into drama 10: Writing a 60-second radio drama script 11: Analysing features of poetry as a genre 12: Writing in the poetic genre	• Learning activity: Genre • Write and assess activity: Descriptive writing • Learning activity: Vocabulary and genre • Learning activity: Drama • Learning activity: Poetry • Worksheet 21a: Exploring genres • Worksheet 21b: Satire
22: Making your writing skills count in the exam	1: Writing and improving an answer to a sample exam question 2: Identifying areas for improvement in own response after peer assessment	• Planning activity: The Writing exam 1 • Connecting comments activity: The Writing exam 2 • On your marks activity: The Writing exam 3
23: Making your writing skills count in the controlled assessment	1: Suggesting possible responses to the 'Prompts and re-creations' task 2: Suggesting ideas for responses to the 'Me. Myself. I.' task 3: Analysing sample responses to the 'Me. Myself. I.' task	• On your marks activity: The Writing controlled assessment 1 • Connecting comments activity: The Writing controlled assessment 2 • Planning activity: The Writing controlled assessment 3 • Worksheet 23a: Basing writing on a poem • Worksheet 23b: Important places

English and English Language Teacher's Book Higher Tier
Section B: Writing

Student checklist worksheet

Read through the following list of skills that you will be expected to demonstrate in your Writing work for GCSE English or GCSE English Language.

Rate your own skills using the columns as a tick chart and then check out which chapters might be most suited to help you tackle any areas you are not sure about.

Skill	Very confident	Quite confident	Sometimes I can	Often I can't	Which chapters might help?
Write in sentences					13
Punctuate sentences correctly					13
Use a range of sentence structures					17
Write in paragraphs					15
Plan and structure my writing					15
Write in a range of non-fiction genres such as emails, letters, news articles					14
Write to suit my audience, purpose and form					14, 16, 17
Adapt language in my writing to suit my audience, purpose and form					14, 16
Use a range of vocabulary in my writing					16
Choose vocabulary to engage my audience and suit my purpose					16
Choose sentences to suit my purpose and communicate clearly and effectively					17, 18, 19
Use different language features to suit my audience and purpose					20
Write in different genres, styles and forms					21
Choose genres, styles and forms to suit my audience and purpose					21

Use your responses to the checklist to set yourself *no more than* three targets to achieve from the Writing section.

1. ....

2. ....

3. ....

Section B
Writing

Checking students' progress

The tasks below are all included in the Student Book and can be used to check student progress in a particular skill.

Chapters	AO focus	Activities from Student Book and learning outcomes
17	- Communicate clearly. - Use a range of sentence structures for clarity, purpose and effect.	**Chapter 13, Activity 10** Students: - identify ambiguity in sentences - rewrite to make them clearer. **Chapter 17, Activity 9** Students: - write one paragraph focusing on varying their sentence structures - use correct punctuation such as commas to make their meaning clear.
14, 20	- Use and adapt form appropriate to task and purpose.	**Chapter 20, Activity 6** Students: - write an article to entertain aimed at a teenage audience - use a range of features to achieve their aims.
15, 18, 19	- Organise information and ideas into structured and sequenced sentences, paragraphs and whole texts; using a variety of linguistic features to support cohesion and overall coherence.	**Chapter 18, Activities 10–11** Students: - plan and write a newspaper article - use a series of paragraphs to structure their article. **Chapter 19, Activity 6 or 8** Students: - use a range of techniques to structure a piece of fiction writing.
21	- Use and adapt form, selecting vocabulary appropriate to task and purpose in ways that engage the reader.	**Chapter 21, Activity 7** Students: - write in two contrasting genres about the same scene - include details relevant to that genre - choose vocabulary relevant to the genre and the atmosphere they want to create.

General resources

The resources in the Student Book, Teacher's Book and *kerboodle!* provide a range of learning opportunities for students and give them practice at developing their skills using a wide variety of text types. The resources suggested below can be used to reinforce, develop and extend students' skills and learning further.

Type of resource	Author and title
Further reading	**Autobiography** Extracts from autobiographies by celebrities are often useful and can be linked with the 'Me. Myself. I.' controlled assessment task. ● David Beckham: *David Beckham: My Side* ● Jade Goody: *Forever in my Heart* ● Peter Kay: *The Sound of Laughter* **Short stories** Extracts from the short stories in the *AQA Anthology* may be useful for practice in identifying varied sentences and the effects created. They can also be used as the starting point for the 'Prompts and re-creations' controlled assessment task. ● Leila Aboulela: 'Something Old, Something New' ● Elizabeth Baines: 'Compass and Torch' ● Helen Dunmore: 'My Polish Teacher's Tie' ● Penelope Lively: 'The Darkness Out There' ● Haruki Murakami: 'On Seeing the 100% Perfect Girl' ● Ridjal Noor: 'Anil' ● Clare Wigfall: 'When the Wasps Drowned' **Poetry** Poems from the *AQA Anthology* can be used as a starting point for students' own poetry writing or for the 'Prompts and re-creations' controlled assessment task. **Preparation texts for the extended writing tasks** Some of these may provide useful themes, such as: children, crime and punishment, families and friendship. These may also offer additional extension reading for students wanting to improve their independent comprehension skills. ● Susan Cooper: *The Dark is Rising* series ● Robert Cormier: *Heroes* ● Philip Pullman: *The Amber Spyglass* ● Robert Swindells: *Stone Cold*
Films/DVDs	● It might be useful to use examples of how the set texts have been recreated in different genres, for example as films or television series. ● *Of Mice and Men*: there are at least two versions of this available which could be used to show how a novel has been transformed into a different genre.
Websites	● Most newspapers have a website on which it is possible to find recent news stories. Alternatively, www.thebigproject.co.uk/news can be used to access a number of local and national newspapers. ● Guidance on writing mini-sagas, along with some examples, can be found at www.britishcouncil.org/learnenglish-central-stories-mini-sagas.htm

13 Getting your message across

AO focus

English AO3 Writing and English Language AO4 Writing.

- Write [to communicate] clearly.

In this chapter your students will:

- develop the skills they need to write clearly for the wider world and for their GCSE exams
- look at writing and punctuating sentences as well as correcting and editing errors.

Additional resources

Worksheets

13a: Making your meaning clear

Getting started

To enable students to focus on different ways of communicating, including non-verbally, you may wish to use the following as a starter activity: adopt a range of different facial expressions and/or poses and ask students to identify what they convey about your mood. Individual students could then be invited to create their own poses for the class to assess.

As an additional activity you could write a range of adverbs on cards and ask for volunteers to perform an action in line with the mood suggested on their card. Suitable adverbs could be:

- angrily
- despairingly
- ecstatically.

Working through the chapter

Depending on the needs of your students, you may wish to work through all the activities in the chapter in order to revise likely problem areas in written communication. An alternative approach could be to focus on different sections as students' revision needs become apparent. For example, before tackling a piece of extended writing you may wish to focus on the punctuation of complex sentences.

Communicating clearly

k! Transformer activity: Writing clearly 1

Activity 1 The aim of this activity is to help students reflect on the numerous ways in which they communicate every day. The results of their partner discussions could be displayed on a 'communication noticeboard' and added to regularly in order to raise continued awareness of how people communicate.

As a homework task students could be invited to bring in examples of written communication for display, for example:

- leaflets
- flyers
- advertisements
- extracts from newspapers or magazine articles
- instructions for using equipment.

As an extension task for this activity you could ask students to work with a partner to make a list of all the reasons why people communicate. This could then be used to annotate the written materials they have collected for display.

Activity 2

a The work on text messaging here could be used alongside Activity 1 from Chapter 14.

b Students could be encouraged to find their own examples of complicated texts and 'translate' them into clearer English along the lines of the work carried out by the Plain English Campaign. Students may find examples in regulations for sports clubs, or in leaflets promoting insurance or bank accounts (Post Office counters are a good source for these).

c Likely reasons are as follows:

- Students send text messages every day – they are very familiar with them.
- They understand all of the abbreviations.
- although the vocabulary of Text B may be familiar, the context is not.

The outcome from this activity is that students will develop awareness of the need for clarity in their own writing in line with the needs of audience and purpose.

Activity 3 There is no set order for the list; the aim here is to focus students on some of the essential features of clear writing, although it is likely that most students will have 'writing in sentences' and 'using full stops and capital letters' near the top of their list.

More able students may begin to reflect on whether it is always necessary to write in full sentences for clear communication: for example, in warning notices such as 'Keep off the grass' and

English and English Language Teacher's Book Higher Tier
Section B: Writing

'No smoking' full sentences would not assist the clarity of the message being communicated.

Sentence sense

Writing in incomplete sentences is a common mistake. This can be particularly apparent when students are writing to describe, when examples such as the following may appear:

- Angry grey clouds moving through the rainy sky.
- A deserted house far away from any other signs of human habitation.

Activity 4 This activity is to remind students of what should be included when writing a complete sentence. For a further challenge, students could be asked to add additional clauses or adverbs to strengthen their understanding of how sentences are built up.

Once the activity has been completed, students could be asked to write a short description of a place (perhaps in response to a picture stimulus) and then to check their own work or the work of a partner to ensure that they have written in complete sentences.

Subject–verb agreement

k! Learning activity: Subject–verb agreement

The aim of this section is to enable students to discuss and reflect on subject–verb agreement which can be a cause of error in writing, particularly when writing under pressure in exams. In Activity 5 the discussion with a partner on the correct form of the verb is intended to raise students' awareness of how to avoid making mistakes in this area in their own writing.

As you are marking and assessing students' work you may wish to build up a list of errors with subject–verb agreement taken from 'live' texts.

Activity 5 Correct answers are:

a My brother and I **were** going on holiday.

   The plural verb is needed because the subject is two people.

b Our team **was** in the lead.

   Although made up of a group of people, 'team' is considered as a single entity.

c Four years **is** a long time to spend away from your friends and family.

   Four years is considered as a single block of time, therefore the singular verb is used.

d He seems to forget there **are** things to be done before he can leave.

   The subject of the verb is the plural 'things'.

e Fish and chips **is** a traditional British dish.

   Fish and chips are considered a single item, that is, one dish.

f James, who **has** returned from holiday in France, **intends** to go back as soon as possible.

   James is a singular subject and therefore a singular verb is used in both cases.

g The best programme on TV last night **was** EastEnders.

   The subject is 'programme' which is singular.

h Maths **is** my favourite subject but my friends all **prefer** Modern Languages.

   'Maths' is a singular subject and 'my friends' is a plural subject.

Getting the tense right

k! Learning activity: Matching tenses

This is an area where even the most able of students can make errors when writing under pressure.

Errors are particularly common in writing to describe or writing to narrate, where students can slip from one tense to another without being aware of it. Once Activity 6 has been completed, students could look back at the short description they wrote in Activity 4 and check whether their tense use has been consistent.

Activity 6 The activity could be completed orally by a student working with a partner.

a

Present tense	Past tense
• hear	• came
• begins	• could see
• takes	• had noticed
• think	• drove
	• recognised

b Students who have chosen to rewrite the text in the present tense could be asked to compare their work with that of students who have chosen the past tense. They could be asked to consider the effects of each:

- The present tense makes the narrative more immediate and suggests the experience is ongoing.
- The past tense records a series of completed events.

c This is intended to get students to reflect on why it is important to be consistent in tense usage. Likely responses are:

- It makes it easier for readers to follow the writer's ideas.

Chapter 13
Getting your message across

- Texts where the tenses are mixed up are confusing for readers.
- If tenses are mixed up, it lessens the impact of the writing.

As an extension activity, more able students could be asked to consider which tenses are conventionally used for different types of writing, for example:

- instructions
- guidebooks
- information texts
- business and personal letters.

Punctuating complex sentences

The control of complex sentence punctuation is a distinct feature of more highly achieving students who have a greater awareness of the impact of their writing on readers. You may find it useful to make a collection of examples of students' writing that are well punctuated as a set of exemplar materials for classroom reference.

Activity 7 Although this activity focuses on the use of commas in complex sentences, you may wish to begin by reminding students that a comma can never be used to end a sentence. Students' own work may well contain examples of comma splices where a comma is used incorrectly to separate sentences.

An important feature of this activity is the discussion between students which will help them to clarify the purpose of using commas to punctuate complex sentences. If students read the sentences aloud it should be clear to them where a comma is needed. This may also help them to understand how commas can be used to create emphasis in a sentence.

- As we all know, being a teenager can be very expensive.
- Even though broccoli was a vegetable she detested, she ate it out of politeness.
- Fighting my instinct to run, I waited until the bear had moved on through the forest.
- The student worked very hard, yet his exam results disappointed him.
- If you dare to walk up the path, you will find the rotting front door inviting you to open it.

Using a range of punctuation

Students should be reminded that the ability to use a full range of punctuation is a skill that is required in writing for both exams and controlled assessment. You may also want to stress to them that the purpose of punctuation is to aid communication for the reader. Giving students a text to read aloud, ignoring all punctuation, followed by a reading of the same text – using punctuation to create pauses and emphasise meaning – should help them to understand this.

Activity 8 You could begin this task by reading the letter aloud and discussing the use of punctuation with the whole class before they write their own texts.

Once they have written their continuation of the letter, students could be asked to annotate the text to indicate where and why they have used punctuation, using the Student Book example as a model.

Making your meaning clear

k! Text transformer activity: Writing clearly 2

This heading sums up the aim of the whole chapter, which is to focus on clarity in communication. Before tackling the activities you could ask students to explain in one sentence why it is important for writers to make their meaning clear. The answer you would expect is that clarity is vital in ensuring that readers can access a text easily and that meaning is fully communicated.

You may also wish to ask students how they can best check that they are communicating clearly. The answer you would expect here is that reading their work aloud and constantly revising and improving is the best way to ensure this.

Activity 9 Students could be asked to find their own examples of ambiguous headlines (the internet is a good source of these) or to write their own following the examples in the Student Book. They could then pass their examples to another student, who could explain the ambiguity and/or rewrite the headline so that the ambiguity is removed.

Activity 10 (Worksheet 13a) Possible versions of rewritten sentences to clear the ambiguity:

- When John was only five, his father married again.
- His grandparents gave him a new car after he graduated from college.
- A policeman and a woman carrying a baby were the only spectators.
- When we were flying from London to Paris we saw the Eiffel Tower.

Students should be able to work out that checking word order is the best way to avoid ambiguity.

Activity 11 (Worksheet 13a) Once they have written their first draft, students could pass their work to a partner for assessment and comments on how they could improve it. The bullet points should be used as the criteria for peer assessment and advice for improvement should be focused around these. Once the text has been revised to incorporate their partner's advice, they could be given to a Year 7 class. Year 7 students could be asked to comment on:

a   the usefulness of the advice

b   how easy it was for them to understand and follow the meaning.

Outcomes

In this chapter your students have:

- thought about what is needed for clear communication
- revised sentence formation and subject–verb agreement
- practised punctuating sentences
- understood how to avoid writing ambiguous sentences.

14 Making the right choices

AO focus

English AO3 Writing and English Language AO4 Writing.

- Write [to communicate] clearly, effectively and imaginatively, using and adapting forms and selecting vocabulary appropriate to task and purpose in ways that engage the reader.

In this chapter your students will:

- explore how they might adapt their use of language to suit audience, purpose and form
- explore non-fiction texts, including aspects of text messaging, emails and letters.

Additional resources

Worksheets

14a: Text messages

Getting started

A preliminary discussion of students' awareness of the differences in language use for mobile phones, email, MSN messaging and conventional school-based writing may be useful. Multi-modal talk – language that blurs the distinction between writing and talking – is an area for controlled assessment in GCSE English Language and it could equally be an interesting focus in GCSE English. There is no requirement to study multi-modal talk in GCSE English for assessment, but a starting discussion, if undertaken in small groups, could form the basis of an interesting Unit 2 assessment.

As a starting point it would be a good idea to:

- compile a list from students of the different forms of written communication they engage in on a daily basis – social networking, text messaging, the variety of school-based writing
- elicit their initial awareness of how their use of language is different in the different forms/media. It would also be a good idea to ask them to talk about how other, older people react to their language use.

Working through the chapter

Text messages

The ways that digital technologies have led to rapid developments in language is a thread that runs through this chapter. It would be a good idea to ascertain students' views of what language use is appropriate in different situations. There is, for example, some evidence to suggest that older teenagers consider text abbreviations/emoticons and so forth to be a little beneath them. The restrictions of 160 characters for text messaging are changing, as messages of more than one page can be created.

Activity 1 An activity based on text messaging may present some difficulties in schools where mobile phones are not allowed and with students who may use their mobile phones for purposes other than those intended. But the maximum length of the task is short enough for the task to be undertaken on a computer or by hand, approaches which also make it easier to display the results to the rest of the class.

The task could be made easier if undertaken with a partner. It will be helpful to suggest that the best results may come from using the informal, abbreviated form of text messaging to express something usually associated with seriousness – the 'Dear Mum' example could be followed by a very serious message, to comic or tragic effect.

Activity 2 (Worksheet 14a) This focuses on an important area for GCSE students. Examiners have reported increasing numbers of examples of candidates using inappropriate language in public examinations. Here are some possible reasons they might give, for and against:

Why it is wrong to use text message language in exams	Why text message language should be allowed in exams
• Public exams must, because they are a standard for the country, be conducted in Standard English. • Variations in non-standard forms of the language make it impossible to assess language use as 'right' or 'wrong'.	• Language changes all the time so the Awarding Bodies should accommodate it. • Exams are about time management and abbreviations allow for quicker responses. • There is no reason why, in a test of reading, candidates' writing skills should be assessed.

It is essential that candidates fully understand, whatever their opinions, that there is an absolute expectation of use of Standard English in GCSE exams.

English and English Language Teacher's Book Higher Tier
Section B: Writing

Emails

Analysis activity: Comparing formality

This section of the chapter focuses on emails and invites students to consider and explore some conventions of the genre. The key teaching point here concerns the importance of audience and purpose. Again, it would be a good idea to discuss student use of email – under what circumstances do they use email?

Activity 3

Learning activity: Formal and informal writing

It would be a good idea to initiate a discussion of the language students use in emails and whether they see it as a formal medium. The list of conventions following the activity is a fairly typical example of its kind. It would be worthwhile discussing the extent to which they follow these conventions: the answer will probably be that it depends on the audience and the purpose. The discussion could be widened to include MSN messaging and to explore why, given the same medium – a keyboard – the kinds of language used may differ.

a They could point out the unconventional punctuation, the use of small 'i', the abbreviated words, the use of capitals to 'shout'.

b Conventional punctuation, correct spelling, complete sentences, letter-writing conventions used.

c Most students will feel that one main reason for the difference concerns age: Text C seems to be written in ways – informal, abbreviated – that are associated with young people, whereas Text D is very formal and uses standard forms of language.

However, it would be good to tease out some ideas which focus on audience and purpose. In the case of Text C the informal chatty style suggests a quite close relationship with the person being written to. Although part of the purpose of Text C is to ask for advice, there is more expression of feeling and the informal language is very expressive and direct in the way it communicates feelings.

Text D on the other hand is very formal and correct and suggests a more distant relationship with the person being written to. The clear purpose of this text is to eventually get some advice for a third party; there is no expression of strong feelings – it is more transactional.

Activity 4

Learning activity: Using language for different audiences and purposes

There may be a variety of responses to the listing activity – the answers are not absolute – but at the more formal end you would expect to find:

- **The email to the small company asking about a placement**: this is because the audience is unknown and adult, and the purpose is serious, requiring a high level of formality.

- **The email to the head of a local company expressing thanks**: this would be formal, especially if the head of the company was largely unknown. Were the head of the company a person the student had been working with, the level of formality would be reduced.

- **The email to the newspaper**: this would probably be quite formal because of the public nature of the medium, but there could be an argument that a newspaper would find a level of informality very acceptable from a young person because it captures the 'voice' of contemporary young people.

At the less formal end, you might expect to find:

- **The email to the form tutor**: this would, in many schools, be quite informal (assuming the form tutor is a well-known, familiar adult), but that depends very much on the ethos of the school, the way the student perceives their relationship with their tutor and, perhaps, the seriousness of the 'problem'.

- **The email to the adult family friend**: this may be a little less informal than the one to a close friend – close friends probably have a shared use of slang and colloquial language.

Activity 5

Analysis activity: Form, audience and purpose

Students should focus on particular aspects of the three responses to the advert:

- **The way the recipient is addressed**: 'To whom it may concern' would be inappropriate because it is over-formal: the advert names 'Gareth Turner', so the named person should be addressed. There may be some debate about the other two choices: the tone of the advert may be considered informal ('get in touch with us') and suggest that 'Hi Gareth' may be acceptable, but 'Dear Mr Turner' would be more appropriate because it does not presume the closeness suggested by 'Gareth'. Use of 'Dear' would be more acceptable than 'Hi' in a situation in which the ethos of the company is unknown.

- **Appropriate use of language**: The language of Text F would be inappropriate for a quite formal form of writing. The use of contractions – 'I'm', 'I've', for example – might be considered informal by some people in

Chapter 14
Making the right choices

the adult world of work. The language of the other two is more formal and therefore more appropriate, but some of the language of Text H could be over-formal. The tone of the original advert is not very formal, so use of words like 'Notwithstanding' could be considered over-formal.

- **How the email is signed off**: Text F would be unwise because the introduction of the nickname assumes a familiarity that is inappropriate. There could be some interesting discussion of the difference between Ms and Miss. Both are acceptable. Students could discuss if a simple 'Lauren Sutcliffe' might be a good idea.

Note: students may not notice the use of 'I'm' in one response and 'I am' in the other two, but it would be a good idea to raise the issue of contractions with them; this may be an area in which the expected level of formality is changing, but in the adult world of business some audiences may expect the more formal response. Just to raise this with students who may not appreciate that it is an issue would be worthwhile.

Letters

Activity 6

a 'and seem unaware'

b 'How often are drivers twiddling the radio controls, adjusting the satnav or, even, talking on a mobile phone?'

c 'just a few cuts and bruises'

d 'My husband is a keen cyclist who has been riding bikes for many years.'

e 'It makes me so cross'

f 'It happens all too often'

g 'Some cyclists may be putting themselves in danger'

Activity 7 Although the letter is based upon a potentially upsetting personal experience that could have been expressed in a quite angry tone as the writer complained bitterly about drivers, Text I is actually written in a very measured tone, which suggests that the writer's purposes were to raise awareness among readers rather than to express anger.

Activity 8 The exemplar paragraph should provide an indication of the techniques that can be employed to change the tone of a piece of writing like this. The focus should be on using some non-standard forms of language to see how they convey different messages from their formal counterparts.

It would be a good idea to put students into small groups to read and assess each other's work, using the criteria that follow 'Make sure that …' in the activity.

Activity 9 It would be useful for students to work in pairs or small groups for this activity. The main focus of the activity is on how language choices create tone, and students are advised to explicitly consider tone before they write the letter. If a pair of students adopted the same 'problem' to which they were responding, they could decide between them to write two letters of contrasting tone: one measured, reasonable, formal and the other angry, sarcastic, with a high level of informality.

Outcomes

In this chapter your students have:

- considered how audience and purpose affect their choice of language
- explored language choices in a variety of non-fiction types.

15 Organising writing

AO focus

English AO3 Writing and English Language AO4 Writing.

- Organise information and ideas into structured and sequenced sentences, paragraphs and whole texts.

In this chapter your students will:

- organise ideas and information into a logical order in sentences and paragraphs
- understand how texts are organised and structured.

Additional resources

Worksheets

15a: Sequencing sentences

15b: Organising sentences into paragraphs

Getting started

As the focus of this chapter is on organisation, a useful starter activity could be to ask students to look at their school planners/homework diaries and to reflect on how they organise their time and the tasks they have to complete. The purpose of this activity would be to make students aware that being organised is not just relevant to writing.

An additional starter activity could be to ask students to look at the organisation of a range of texts and to comment on their organisation – for example, the use of headlines in newspapers or the relationship between images and texts in promotional materials.

Working through the chapter

It is preferable to work through this chapter in order, as the progression of activities begins at sentence level, working through to organisation within paragraphs, thus enabling students to understand how the organisation of ideas works within texts.

Sequencing sentences

Activity 1

Learning activity: Organising information

(Worksheet 15a) This activity enables students to reflect on how ideas are linked within a text and to produce a logical order for the sentences. Before they begin the task you may wish to discuss the content of the bullet points with students, to clarify the logical processes behind the order of sentences in a text.

It is not important that all students have the same order for the sentences, as long as their version makes sense. You could ask students to justify the order they have chosen, using the bullet points as criteria. It is to be hoped that students will work out in their own discussions that the order of sentences can vary, thus reinforcing the idea that as writers they have choices to make about the organisation of their ideas. If they do not manage to reach this conclusion it would be helpful to point it out to them.

The order from the original article is as follows: 3, 6, 2, 1, 4, 5.

Activity 2

Before starting the activity you could ask students to discuss with a partner what they like about holidays.

Once they have written five sentences, students could pass their work to a partner to check that the ideas are in a logical sequence.

Organising sentences into paragraphs

The aim of this section is to help students examine in detail how ideas are organised in paragraphs and how one paragraph links with another. The aim is to enable them to understand how cohesion works within a text, with ideas from one paragraph being continued and developed in another.

Activity 3 (Worksheet 15b) Before studying the text closely your students could identify the key points orally, either in small groups or as a whole class.

The following are likely responses to the questions:

a The main topic of the article (plastic bags) is referred to in the heading and in the opening paragraph.

b The focus in this paragraph is on the sea turtles. The linking words are 'plastic bags'.

c The 'similarly painful death' of the minke whale refers back to the death of the turtles mentioned in paragraphs 3 and 4.

d In paragraph 6 words and phrases which refer to:

  (i) plastic bags are 'they', 'flimsy bags'

  (ii) their long life are 'will take up to 1,000 years to rot away'.

Chapter 15
Organising writing

e The damage to seabirds and animals, causing their death, was first referred to in paragraph 2.

f The final paragraph of the article refers back to the title and to the campaign to ban plastic bags which the *Daily Mail* is sponsoring.

Linking ideas within a paragraph

Learning activity: Organised writing

Activity 4

a The activity enables students to see how cohesion works in one paragraph – particularly through the use of pronouns.

b The topic developed in paragraph 6 is the long life of plastic bags. Other words used by the writer to refer to the bags in the paragraph are:
- flimsy bags
- by-product of crude oil
- they
- them.

Activity 5

Write and assess activity: Writing cohesively

The aim of this activity is to reinforce what students have learned so far about sequencing ideas within and between paragraphs. It also gives them the chance to practise what they have learned about text cohesion by linking words and phrases within their text.

The peer assessment is an important feature of this activity as it enables students to have their text cohesion checked by another reader.

Once students have redrafted their work you may want to use some pieces for classroom display, annotated to show how text cohesion is exemplified.

Understanding writers' techniques

The purpose of this section is to help students understand how vocabulary and linguistic techniques can add cohesion to a text. The extract enables them to see how a writer develops a metaphor throughout the course of a paragraph.

Activity 6

Analysis activity: How texts hang together

Any valid responses based on the text should be accepted, but likely answers to questions are as follows:

- **How does the writer indicate the fire is just beginning?**
  'Smoke was rising here and there' – may also refer to 'a flash of fire', 'small flames'.

- **What effect does the word 'crawled' create for the reader?**
  The word 'crawled', uses to describe flames, could make the reader think of a comparison with an animal, or could make them think the fire is building up slowly and gradually. It could make readers think the fire is like a living creature.

- **Why do you think the writer uses the simile of the spreading fire being like a squirrel? What effects did the writer want to achieve?**
  Squirrels can be red like the colour of flames; squirrels also dart about quickly. The writer may want to help the reader to appreciate the speed with which the fire is developing.

- **Why has the writer used the metaphor 'wings of the wind'? What effect does this metaphor convey?**
  The wings of the wind suggests that the wind is carrying the flames through the trees, and helps the reader to appreciate the speed with which the fire is spreading.

- **What vocabulary does the writer use to develop the image of the squirrel in the rest of the paragraph?**
  'Leapt' and 'clung'.

- **Why is the use of the word 'gnaw' appropriate? What is the effect of using this as the final word in the paragraph?**
  The word 'gnaw' to describe the action of the fire taking hold is appropriate because it is a word normally used to describe a squirrel's nibbling action. It suggests that the fire is encroaching on the forest.

Activity 7 The purpose of asking students to write a short paragraph is to enable them to craft their writing carefully.

In order to assist students with the development of ideas, you could give them a thesaurus and set a short time limit for them to find vocabulary connected with one or even two of the suggested topics for writing: heavy rain, a blizzard, a storm or extreme heat. Once they have chosen suitable vocabulary, it may be easier for students to think of appropriate comparisons.

You should remind them of the importance of planning their work, even when writing a relatively small text. There are opportunities here for peer assessment after the initial planning stage, when students may welcome advice on additional vocabulary to use or on how to create and develop a comparison. Once the first draft has been written, the same partner could check the paragraph and offer advice for improvement before the final draft is written. The peer assessor should check that the comparison is sustained throughout the paragraph, as in Text B.

An alternative approach to this task could be to allow students to work with a partner to collaborate on their paragraph. They could then have their work peer-assessed by another pair of students.

Activity 8 In this activity students learn how vocabulary can be used to create mood and tone throughout a paragraph.

Likely answers to the questions are as follows:

a Students may say that the atmosphere created is depressing.

b The word 'black' creates a dismal, gloomy mood.

c Other words that reflect this are 'dreadful', 'stink', 'hard', 'dim', 'threatening'.

d The words 'even darker than usual' suggest that there is something, possibly something bad, which is causing the girl's eyes to look this way. This makes the reader want to read on to discover why.

e Students may wish to use a thesaurus to select a range of vocabulary to create a happy and joyful mood. They could also compare their rewritten versions with those of a partner.

Activity 9 This is an extension of the skills used in Activity 7. Here the students are asked to develop their writing over three paragraphs, giving them further opportunity to organise and develop their ideas in a coherent way, using vocabulary to create a specific mood. As with all writing, the planning stages are crucial to the production of a coherent final piece.

The peer assessment is an important stage of the writing process, as it enables students to reflect on advice from others and to refine and improve their writing. It may be useful if the student carrying out the peer assessment uses a highlighter to trace the development of ideas or of a particular type of vocabulary, as in this example:

> Grey, dismal-looking clouds scudded across the dreary sky. At this time of the evening, on a bitterly cold winter's day, the streets were empty of people – that is, until an old man appeared on the corner.

A typical comment from a peer assessor could be: your vocabulary creates a bleak mood at the beginning of this paragraph, but you need to continue with this. Could you find some different vocabulary to describe the street and the old man?

Once students' work has been redrafted you may wish to select some for display, with appropriate annotations to indicate how mood and atmosphere have been sustained.

Outcomes

In this chapter your students have:

- considered how sentences can be organised in a logical sequence
- examined how sentences are organised into paragraphs
- studied how ideas are linked within a paragraph
- worked out how writers use a range of techniques to connect meanings within a paragraph
- explored how words can be used to create atmosphere.

16 Getting the words right

AO focus

English AO3 Writing and English Language AO4 Writing.

- Write [to communicate] clearly, effectively and imaginatively, using and adapting forms and selecting vocabulary appropriate to task and purpose in ways that engage the reader.

In this chapter your students will:

- use a range of vocabulary through example and exploration
- engage an audience through vocabulary choices.

Additional resources

Worksheets

16a: Writing techniques 1
16b: Writing techniques 2

Getting started

The focus in this chapter is on vocabulary choices, especially in descriptive writing. Much of the chapter invites students to focus on a particularly interesting and quite unusual descriptive passage, but the opening activities suggest some experimentation with vocabulary based on smaller models of descriptive writing.

Students should be told that the focus will be on the importance of selecting the right word to create effects on the reader. They need to be aware of the huge range of words potentially at their disposal.

A light-hearted way to begin the focus on individual words could be to put students into small groups/teams and to set up a quick competition. Ask for a list of words that could replace 'said' in the phrase 'She said'. Give 60 seconds for groups to write down as many words as they can think of. This could be repeated with 'He looked at the girl.' What words could replace 'looked'? Make the simple point that there are invariably choices to be made.

Working through the chapter

Selecting vocabulary

Activity 1 This informal starter activity is intended to focus on the details of individual words rather than, for example, plot. A variation of the idea is to write something avoiding a particular vowel (or two). Different students could be given different vowels to include or avoid – it would bring some variety when results are shared. No more than 10 or 15 minutes should be devoted to the activity.

Choosing from a variety of words

Learning activity: Choosing vocabulary 1

This activity builds on what the class did as a starter activity. It moves beyond simple lists and invites students to categorise words to show that it is not simply the case that there are lots of words of movement; there are lots of words to describe fast movement, slow movement, and so on.

Activity 2 Some students may need to be reminded about/introduced to the idea of the thesaurus.

a–c Words of movement provide a wide choice. Some variety could be introduced by giving alternatives to the class before they focus on words of movement. There could be 60 seconds each on words of:

- seeing/looking
- hitting
- speaking.

d There could be elegant/graceful words, dramatic words, subtle words, painful words, energetic words, words associated with age, words associated with childhood.

The results could form a useful display to act as a simple reminder of the possibility of vocabulary choices.

It might be a good idea to display understanding of the different shades of meaning of words by following the examples on page 100 of the Student Book. Students are given three examples (starting with 'he swaggered') of how individual words could be expressed differently. They could attempt the same with two or three other words from their lists.

Activity 3 Students can explore a variety of sentence structures in Chapter 17 of the Student Book and it would be helpful if they had a grasp of subordinate clauses. A grasp of the terminology ('present participle' is another term used) is not, however, essential – most students will understand the method of adding information to the main part of the sentence.

It might be a good idea to demonstrate unwise/ unnecessary choice of simile:

- Like a ballroom dancer she danced along the corridor.

67

English and English Language Teacher's Book Higher Tier
Section B: Writing

Students could discuss whether a construction which is basically, 'Like a dancer she danced' is effective. It could be compared with:

- Like a ballroom dancer she glided along the corridor.

The activity could be undertaken with a partner.

Students could be invited to select the example they think is most effective and share it with the rest of the class. It may also be a good idea to invite them to share examples that do not work – it will help them to be explicit about the effect of vocabulary choices.

Creating tone

k! Learning activity: Choosing vocabulary 2

The example builds on the work students did in Activity 3. The opening sentence of Text B uses the present participle/simile construction that students attempted, but adds further detail.

Students should be focused on how the choice of vocabulary in the opening sentence creates a comic tone: the word 'slaloming' may need to be explained, and it may be profitable to mention another possibility – 'weaving'. The word may mean something very similar, but does not have the same effect because it does not introduce the idea of skiing, a sport associated with youth and gracefulness, and is therefore very inappropriate for Mrs Jenkins.

Before students attempt Activity 4, they could be asked to change the tone of the opening sentence to something more serious. For example:

- Stumbling slowly down the street, her stick shaking uncertainly, Mrs Jenkins slowly approached the Post Office.

The details are the same, but the change of vocabulary changes the tone.

Activity 4 Like other activities, this could be attempted with a partner. The description of Mrs Jenkins could be used as a template by some students. It may help to present students with a menu of possible situations, for example:

- an arrogant young man swaggering along a street
- a shifty character sneaking around in the twilight
- a nervous young person on their way to an interview
- a young mother pushing an angry toddler in a pushchair.

Writing techniques

In this section students will explore the ways a writer has made particularly interesting vocabulary choices to create a vivid description. The focus is on sounds and it would be worthwhile pointing out to students before they begin that most descriptive writing concerns sight. Their own writing could be made more interesting if they use a wider range of senses.

Activity 5 (Worksheet 16a) There are several words used to describe sound in the extract (and there are also many words of movement that could be identified):

- sings
- low soothing hum
- a lullaby hum
- engines rumbling
- clack-clacking like cast-iron castanets
- the fizzing hiss
- shouting
- the hard crash and ring and clatter
- shrill-calling
- a hammered ring like a lightning drum-roll
- a mesmeric bell-toll
- crying
- babies waawaa-ing
- sung sirens
- the slow wail
- a lament
- sing
- blurting hey and rumbling
- hoots
- shouts
- hums
- crackles
- humming.

Some students may require some extra support with the paragraph in the Student Book concerning the sounds of words. Some may need help to grasp the distinction between long and short vowel sounds, as well as hard and soft consonant sounds.

Activity 6 For '… drains and manhole covers clack-clacking like cast-iron castanets', students should notice the use of the short 'a' vowel sound and the repeated use of the hard 'c'/'ck' consonant sound.

Chapter 16
Getting the words right

For '… Sung sirens, sliding through the streets, streaking blue light', students should notice the long vowel sounds of 'i' and the repeated use of the soft 's' sound.

Activity 7 The six similes are:

- 'clack-clacking like cast-iron castanets'
- 'shouting to each other like drummers in rock bands calling out rhythms'
- 'a hammered ring like a lightning drum-roll'
- 'like a mesmeric bell-toll'
- 'crying their needs to the night like an understaffed orphanage'
- 'all come together and rouse like a choir'.

The odd one out is the one about an orphanage because the other five concern music/instruments.

Activity 8 (Worksheet 16b) Some possible responses are given in the table at the bottom of the page.

Organising the description

Activity 9

a Each paragraph begins with a statement of which part of the city landscape/soundscape will be the focus.

b This could be linked to the work on the paragraph about Mrs Jenkins, when the writer created effects by compressing a lot of detail into single sentences. By adding layers of detail in the same sentence the writer emphasises the huge amount of life and variety of sound in the city. It is also a quite complex and sustained description, and the single sentence makes it easier for the reader to plot their way through it.

Activity 10 Students should write a single long sentence, like the example beginning 'Restless machines …' Examples should be displayed and shared.

Activity 11 This is an activity intended to give students the opportunity to show what they have learned from the chapter: they should remind themselves of the 'Concentrate on …' points before they start.

It would be a good idea to use peer assessment here. Students should read a partner's text and comment on the effectiveness of the writing in:

- choosing words for their sounds
- use of similes
- use of listing
- variety of sentence structures.

Outcomes

Analysis activity: Word choices 1

Text transformer activity: Word choices 2

In this chapter your students have:

- explored the effects of different vocabulary choices
- experimented with different ways of structuring vocabulary.

Metaphor	Explanation
'Lullaby hum'	This is a metaphor because air-conditioning machines don't actually hum lullabies – only humans can do that. The writer uses the metaphor to suggest that there is something very soothing about the sound of air-conditioning units at night; they can lull you into sleep.
'Road menders … pasting new skins on the veins of the city.'	The metaphor here is that road-mending is compared to a medical procedure: the city is a living entity and the road menders, like doctors, patch up wounds. This makes the ordinary, the commonplace, seem special, but the main effect is that it reinforces the idea of the city being alive.
'And all the alarms … crying their needs to the night.'	The comparison here is that alarms are compared to the cries of people in distress, especially, at the end of the paragraph, of babies in distress. The effect is, again, to reinforce the idea of the city being alive.
'the cars blurting hey and rumbling all headlong'	The cars seem to be compared to people – 'blurting hey' sounds like they are saying hello to each other. In the absence of people, in the middle of the night, describing machines like cars as though they are people emphasises the living, breathing nature of the city.

17 Making sense of sentences

AO focus

English AO3 Writing and English Language AO4 Writing.

- Use a range of sentence structures for clarity, purpose and effect.

In this chapter your students will:

- practise using a range of sentence structures
- match their sentence structures to the audience and purpose of their text
- express their ideas clearly, emphasise their meaning and create effects for their readers.

Additional resources

Worksheets

17a: Creating patterns: lists and repetitions

Getting started

A useful starter could be to ask students to list what they already know about sentences, based on their work in Chapter 13. They could then add to the list other facts that they know about sentences, for example, different types of sentences.

As an additional starter you could give students a highlighter and ask them to mark different types of sentences in a newspaper article. If you set a specific time limit for this of 5–10 minutes, the students will focus on the task and are less likely to be distracted by reading the newspaper.

Working through the chapter

The initial activities in the chapter are intended as a revision of different sentence types. The main focus of this chapter is to give students practice in selecting appropriate sentence structures linked to the audience and purpose of a text.

Sentence types

If this has not already been covered in a starter activity, you could begin by asking students if they can list the four main sentence types referred to in the Student Book. Once the four sentence types have been identified, you may wish to extend students further by asking them to list examples of texts where these sentence types might occur. Perhaps they may say that a quiz or an exam paper would use a range of questions. Exclamations are sometimes used quite frequently in children's stories.

You may also wish to ask them to consider the effect of using too many sentences of the same type in one text. For example, if too many imperatives are used in an advice text, the tone becomes too abrupt and readers are less likely to follow the advice.

Sentence structures

Learning activity: Sentence structures

For many students this section will be revision and you may wish them to complete the activities orally. As an extension activity or a homework task, you could ask them to investigate the sentence structures of a similar range of texts (children's story, recipe, holiday advertisement) to ascertain whether or not similar sentence structures are used. If different sentence structures are used, students could be asked to work out the reasons for this. For example, a story for older children might use a wider range of sentence structures than one for very young children.

Activity 1 Students may find other valid purposes for the texts, for example, they may say that Text C informs or describes. However, likely responses are as follows:

Text	Intended reader	Intended purpose
Text A	young children	to entertain
Text B	adults/young people	to instruct
Text C	adults	to persuade

Activity 2 The purpose of this activity is to enable students to reflect on the reasons why writers choose to use a particular sentence structure. Likely answers are as follows:

a Sentence structures used are simple sentences to make it easy for young children to understand the story.

b The main sentence type is an imperative/directive, so that the series of instructions can be expressed clearly and directly.

c The writer may have chosen to use complex sentences in order to combine a range of information in relatively few sentences.

Considering audience and purpose

The aim here is to reinforce for students that the sentence structure of a text is closely related to

Chapter 17
Making sense of sentences

the needs of the audience as well as the purpose of a text.

Activity 3 The purpose of this activity is to provide practice in reorganising the sentence structure of a text to match audience and purpose.

A reorganised text may look something like this:

> Carnivorous plants, which are also known as insectivorous plants, can trap insects or spiders for food. The plants grow in places with poor soil which does not contain many nutrients (food for the plants), for example, bogs or rocky outcrops.
>
> Different plants have different ways of trapping the insects. Some plants are pitcher plants and when the insects fall into the pitcher they cannot escape. Other plants use 'flypaper' traps which can secrete a sticky glue, trapping the insect on the leaves of the plant.

This version contains a simple sentence, a compound sentence and complex sentences.

You may wish to ask students to annotate their own work or the work of another student to indicate which sentence structures have been used.

Creating emphasis and variety

Learning activity: Sentence effects

After completing the following activity, students should have developed greater awareness of how using a variety of sentences can make a text more interesting for the reader.

Activity 4 The focus of this activity is to enable students to understand that using a variety of sentences can make a text more interesting for the reader. The model text is an advice text written in a conversational tone, using a range of sentence structures to create variety and to soften the tone of the advice.

Students should be encouraged to discuss their ideas with a partner or plan on paper before writing the continuation. One purpose of the peer assessment is to raise awareness of sentence structures.

Creating patterns: lists and repetitions

Analysis activity: Sentence patterns

In this section students are made aware of how organising sentences in a particular way can have considerable effect on the reader. The effect of lists and repetitions on the reader can best be tested by reading aloud. You may wish to encourage students to adopt this practice wherever practical when writing first drafts, as this helps them to consider their writing from the point of view of the reader.

You may wish to point out that the sentence structures used here form part of the conventions of rhetoric. More able students may be able to make links with other rhetorical texts they may have read, such as Old Major's speech from *Animal Farm*.

Activity 5 (Worksheet 17a) Students are asked to focus on a range of sentence patterns so that they can use similar patterns in their own writing in the following activity.

Likely responses are included in the table at the bottom of the page.

Activity 6 You may also wish to ask students to perform the opening of their speeches as an oral activity in order to test the impact of their rhetorical sentence structures.

Members of the class acting as an audience could be asked to note down examples of the sentence patterns from Activity 5.

Using sentence structure to create effects

The focus now is on using a range of sentence structures within a piece of narrative writing.

Sentence pattern	Example	Idea the writer wants to emphasise
Repetition of sentence beginning/endings	... the change we need doesn't come from Washington. Change comes to Washington. Change happens ...	Change is now inevitable in the United States and will come not from the government but from the people
Repetition of similar structures in one sentence	... because I've seen it, because I've lived it.	He has personal experience of such change
Using words or phrases in groups of three	new ideas, new leadership, a new politics ...	Underlines the main idea of the speech that if elected Obama would bring a fresh approach to the presidency

71

English and English Language Teacher's Book Higher Tier
Section B: Writing

Students should be made aware of the impact these sentences have on the reader – again, reading aloud may help here. Before tackling the questions around the text, students could be asked to read Text G aloud with a partner, noting how the sentence structures vary and considering the effect on the reader.

If students do not discover this for themselves, you may wish to point out:

- the effect of short sentences, which cause the reader to wonder what will follow and create some tension
- the sentence patterning in the sentence beginning 'She never told me …'.

Activity 7 Likely responses to the questions are as follows:

- **Who does this sentence focus on? How does it help to draw the reader into the girl's experience?**
  The sentence focuses on the girl looking at what is before her. It draws the reader in as they want to find out what she is staring at.

- **What has the writer done to build up tension in this sentence?**
  The writer has used a three-part compound sentence to help build the tension.

- **How does this short sentence prepare the reader for the next section of the text?**
  'Soon the great stones faded' closes that part of the story and prepares the reader for something new.

- **This is the final sentence in the chapter. What effect might it have on the reader?**
  The short simple sentence 'beyond that all was black' finishes the chapter on a note of drama and mystery.

Activity 8 Here students are given an opportunity to craft their writing carefully and to consider how sentence structure can contribute to the overall effect. They should be encouraged to use the sentence structures of Text G as a model. You may wish to remind them of the sentence structures they have observed in this text:

- short sentences for effect
- verbal patterning as in 'She never told me …'.

There are opportunities here for peer assessment, where students are asked to highlight examples of both of the above in a partner's work. They could also give a star rating of one to three (the best) to indicate how well their partner has created tension and built up to the final sentence.

Punctuating sentences

The focus here is on the use of commas within sentences – something that many students find difficult. Before completing the activity students could be asked to find examples of the use of the comma within a sentence, perhaps by looking at other texts in the Student Book. They could be asked to explain why they think the comma has been used in their examples.

Activity 9 The point of this activity is to make students reflect on how the use of commas can influence the way the reader reads a text. Explaining their use of the comma to other students should reinforce the idea that writers need to think about the needs of their readers when punctuating their work.

Controlling the pace of your writing

Controlling the pace of writing through the use of punctuation is a skill that needs developing in all but the most able of students. The model provided can be used by students to improve their own practice. As before, reading the text aloud will enable students to appreciate the effect of the punctuation for the reader.

Stretch yourself

This is intended as an extension activity for students who are already confident writers with good sentence control. It could be offered as an alternative to Activity 9. Some ideas that students could develop are as follows:

- the advantages of having a holiday job
- taking up a new sport, such as rock climbing/ scuba diving, in order to develop a sense of adventure
- finding interesting and rewarding voluntary work
- travelling with friends to explore different parts of the UK.

Outcomes

Connecting comments activity: Using a range of sentences in writing

Text transformer activity: Combining sentences

In this chapter your students have:

- revised a range of sentence structures
- chosen sentences to suit their audience and purpose
- used a range of sentences to create an impact on their readers
- used punctuation in sentences to control the pace of their writing.

18 Getting it together 1: non-fiction writing

AO focus

English AO3 Writing and English Language AO4 Writing.

- Organise information and ideas into structured and sequenced sentences, paragraphs and whole texts, using a variety of linguistic and structural features to support cohesion and overall coherence.

In this chapter your students will:

- focus on the importance of structure in their writing
- explore ways of planning and organising their non-fiction writing
- explore different ways of structuring texts.

Additional resources

Worksheets

18a: Planning your writing
18b: Structuring your writing

Getting started

This chapter focuses on structure. The absence of thoughtful whole-text structure is something that often restricts the achievement of GCSE students. In Unit 1, students will have to produce two pieces of writing in only 1 hour, and it is important that they have a good grasp of ways of planning and structuring writing. In Unit 3, one of the three main strands of the controlled assessment criteria is called 'Organising information and ideas', and to achieve Band 3 students must use 'clear and distinctive organisational devices'; there must be a 'clear sense of whole text coherence'.

It is worthwhile beginning by raising the importance of paragraphing. Students could be asked some simple questions:

- **What is a paragraph?**
  A group of sentences about one idea.

- **What would cause you to finish one paragraph and start a new one?**
  Moving on to a new idea or stage of an argument.

- **What are discourse markers?**
  Words used to link different parts of a piece of writing.

Students could be asked to think of alternative words to a discourse marker which:

- moves an argument forward (such as 'furthermore', 'moreover', 'in addition')
- introduces a contrasting idea (such as 'nonetheless', 'however', 'nevertheless')
- connects the next paragraph logically to the previous one (such as 'therefore', 'subsequently', 'as a result').

Use of discourse markers is specifically mentioned in assessment criteria, so it is worthwhile making sure students are aware of their variety and significance.

Working through the chapter

Planning your writing

Activity 1 Ideas about and methods of planning should be shared. A starting point for discussion about planning might be to give a task to small groups, for example:

- Your school is to compile a concise school prospectus for prospective parents. It needs to be divided into sections. What section headings would you have, and in what order would you put them?

The responses could be shared to illustrate that there can be a variety of plans, and a general question could be discussed: Why does a text like a school prospectus require planning?

The response: 'I don't plan my writing, I just do it' is fairly commonplace. It would be worthwhile airing the views of the reluctant planners to identify and confront the negatives. Any 'problems' should be written down.

Activity 2 Most students will say that the essential elements of the story have been established by the end of the third paragraph, perhaps even by the end of the second. It is certainly possible to make almost complete sense of the story by the end of the second paragraph, although it is not completely made clear until the third paragraph that the girl lived at home.

The point to be made clear to students is that the shape of the writing has been planned so that important information goes first.

It might be a good idea to let students discuss how the story could be restructured for a different kind of purpose. If the story began: '"They never let her out, we didn't know she existed," said one neighbour', it might not be an effective news

73

story, but it would introduce the kind of suspense associated with different kinds of stories.

Activity 3

a   The practical answer will focus on the needs of editors to be easily able to cut stories. Another answer will be that it makes the story easier to read. If students are unfamiliar with the idea of 'tabloid paragraphs', it would be a good idea – and helpful for their exam work – to explore ideas of audience and purpose surrounding the use of single-sentence paragraphs, and their merits and drawbacks.

b   The 'girl of five' becomes 'Natasha', then 'she', then 'her', then 'this child', before finally becoming 'the girl'. There is a simple but important point to be made about ways of introducing 'variety' into writing.

Activity 4 Some students might say the key part of the story ends at the end of the sixth paragraph, though others might argue it is more at the end of the eighth (when the fact that the bull ran out of the store is given). They will notice that the eyewitness accounts, the quotations, are only used in the later stages of the story.

Activity 5

a   This reinforces Activity 3. Breaking stories down into small units helps readers to follow them. It also helps newspaper editors – on a practical level, it helps them rearrange space.

b   This activity is intended to show that there are choices when it comes to paragraphing a piece of writing; there is more than one way of doing it. It may be worthwhile discussing why 'quality' newspapers may have multi-sentence paragraphs (not losing sight, however, of the considerable number of single-sentence paragraphs in the 'quality' press). This discussion should be made relevant to the Reading section of Unit 1: in their exam, students need the skill to 'explain and evaluate how writers use linguistic, grammatical, structural and presentational features'. A discussion of single-sentence paragraphs should explore why writers might choose to use them – to draw attention to a particular key idea by putting it in a short, single-sentence paragraph, in contrast to longer paragraphs; to suit a potential target audience; to suit a particular reading context – newspapers are often read as people are travelling, read in snatches.

There should be discussion, for example, of why it would be possible to group the first three sentences into one paragraph: they concern the essence of the complete story. The fourth, fifth and sixth paragraphs could be joined as a more detailed look at the events before the eyewitness account is introduced.

Activity 6 (Worksheet 18a) When the stories are finished the different sections could be shaded in different colours to show explicitly where the different sections are.

The two main purposes of this activity are to:

- provide practice in the idea of an hourglass structure
- move students on from one-sentence, tabloid paragraphing.

It would make for more interesting feedback if students made up their own stories. If they do, they should be encouraged to fill in a simple table in the same way as the story in the book.

Structuring your writing

This part of the chapter looks at ways of organising non-fiction writing into sections/paragraphs.

Activity 7 (Worksheet 18b)

a   The correct order is 2, 4, 1, 3.

b   This should not take long. Students will notice features of vocabulary used by the writer to give shape to the writing, for example:

- how (2) establishes a setting and ends on a sentence that clearly indicates a future experience
- how 'The outlook' follows on from the 'revelation' at the end of the first paragraph
- the sentence 'Not just any fox' clearly picks up from '– a fox'.
- the opening sentence of (3) could only come after the setting and the fox had been established. A key feature is the way the writer uses the detail of the prosecco to remind the reader of the way the piece started: it is a satisfying conclusion to this concise piece of writing.

c   The word 'prosecco'. Having been used by the writer in the opening paragraph, it is used again to emphasise the writer's sense of celebration at having seen the fox.

Activity 8 (Worksheet 18b) Students will grasp the structure quite easily. They may need more help with generating ideas. It would be a good idea to collect a range of thoughts that could emerge from the simple action of seeing an animal. One example is given in the book. Others might include:

- the beauty, grace of animals
- how animals are like humans in some respects
- how the simple things in life are often the best
- the rawness or cruelty of the natural world.

Chapter 18
Getting it together 1: non-fiction writing

Writer's sentence	Comment
How can this be?	A short sentence which shows the reader that the writer is about to engage with the issue of the first paragraph (Text D).
In my work I visit hundreds of schools and meet thousands of boys who read, pass exams, live normal lives.	A leisurely sentence, controlled by the commas, which stresses the 'normality' of the lives of most young people. He is responding to the question in his opening sentence.
I have given out Duke of Edinburgh awards to kids who have shamed me with their energy and generosity.	He is emphasising his point about normality by adding another detail which is a response to his opening question.
None of these are ever reported.	A deliberately short sentence which makes his point following the two longer sentences.
And although, yes, 27 knife murders in London in one year is an appalling statistic, we all know in our hearts that this a terrible variegation, not the golden rule.	He finishes the paragraph by explicitly drawing out the point he has been developing in the first four sentences.

Activity 9 The correct order is:
- How can this be?
- In my work I visit hundreds of schools and meet thousands of boys who read, pass exams, live normal lives.
- I have given out Duke of Edinburgh awards to kids who have shamed me with their energy and generosity.
- None of these are ever reported.
- And although, yes, 27 knife murders in London in one year is an appalling statistic, we all know in our hearts that this a terrible variegation, not the golden rule.

A commentary might include some of the point given in the table at the top of the page.

Activity 10 Generating ideas could be an individual task or it could be undertaken in a small-group or whole-class discussion. As small-group discussion it could be a useful opportunity for a Discussing and listening assessment.

Activity 11 Students should read the response of another student and appraise its effectiveness:
- Does it have a purposeful, concise opening?
- Is each subsequent paragraph devoted to a separate idea?
- Does the final paragraph conclude the writing concisely and sum up the main idea of the article?

Stretch yourself
Although no extension activity is given in the Student Book, it would be useful to collect and display examples of discourse markers – as many as possible. Lists could be found on a simple internet search. A useful activity would be to ask individual students to exemplify the use of different discourse markers by writing two paragraphs on a topic, beginning the second paragraph with whichever discourse marker they are given from the class-compiled list. These could be displayed on a classroom wall, with the discourse markers highlighted or marked in a different colour to stand out. The display would help to remind the class about text structure.

Outcomes

Planning activity: Argumentative writing

Planning activity: Informative writing

In this chapter your students have:
- explored different kinds of planning
- explored different ways of structuring their non-fiction writing.

19 Getting it together 2: fiction writing

AO focus

English AO3 Writing and English Language AO4 Writing.

- Organise information and ideas into structured and sequenced sentences, paragraphs and whole texts, using a variety of linguistic and structural features.
- Write [to communicate] clearly, effectively and imaginatively.

In this chapter your students will:

- explore different ways of structuring and planning their imaginative writing.

Additional resources

Worksheets

19a: Planning a story based on a photograph

Getting started

Chapter 18 focused on organising non-fiction writing. In this chapter students will explore a range of ways of structuring imaginative writing. In Unit 3 of GCSE English, students will produce two pieces of imaginative writing in controlled assessment, and one of the key assessment criteria by which their writing will be assessed concerns whole-text organisation. In the preparation and planning stage of the controlled assessment tasks, it will be important to ensure that students consider different ways of structuring their writing.

The chapter begins with an exercise in very concise writing; it could be useful to get students thinking about structure by giving them the challenge of coming up with five-noun story outlines.

- For example: man ... spaceship ... planet ... alien ... death.

The five nouns establish a basic story and the order could be changed:

- For example: planet ... alien ... spaceship ... man ... death.

A flashback structure could be introduced by starting with 'death'.

Students could be asked to invent their own five-noun story outlines, to be shared with the class. They could be asked to explore the possibilities of changing the order of the five nouns.

Working through the chapter

Imaginative writing

Activity 1

Learning activity: Mini-saga

Although this activity means students only have to write 50 words, it is a quite difficult task, made more challenging by the requirement to begin and end with 'opposites'.

The only sensible place to begin is with an idea, something that could be developed from a pair of opposites. It may be worthwhile spending some time exploring different possibilities. For example, black/white could lead to a story about:

- racial harmony
- racial disharmony
- a pianist
- despondency growing into hope.

It is a good idea to write an approximation of 50 words first, something that can be used as a draft for pruning or additions: it is a good way to focus on precise vocabulary choices, as students realise that there is, for example, a single word that can effectively replace a phrase.

Titles can be as long as students wish, and can be very effective in adding meaning.

Students will focus on the mathematical challenge of writing the 50 words, but when they have finished the key focus should be on structure – the way they have moved from one word to its opposite.

Organising writing chronologically

This section of the chapter begins with straight-forward ways of organising a narrative – telling the story in chronological fashion. This is the obvious, logical way of telling any story, so it could be worthwhile asking students why any storyteller might choose NOT to tell a story chronologically.

Activity 2 It would be best if the sentences were based on real memories, but the point – constructing effective opening sentences to draw a reader in – could just as easily be made by inviting 'creative' responses intended to surprise a reader, for example:

- 'The first time I discovered the ability to fly, I was seven years old, lying in my sleeping bag under canvas in the Lake District.'

This could be an effective opening to a story about an accident-prone child.

Activity 3

Learning activity: Writing descriptively

a The answers are:
- 'the local church of St Vincent de Paul'
- 'a dusty, sun-bleached London Saturday afternoon in high summer'
- 'a pyramid-shaped lump of frozen orange squash called a Jubbly'
- 'the slimy, orange-silted bits of cardboard'
- 'some icy shards of squash'.

Although the focus of the chapter is on whole-text structure, the use of noun phrases is an obvious feature of the passage and a quite straightforward technique for students, especially higher-tier students, to grasp and employ in their own writing.

b The answers are:
- 'dusty, sun-bleached'
- 'in high summer, so hot'
- 'like twin ovens round your baking feet'
- 'your raging thirst'
- 'frozen orange squash'
- 'icy shards of squash'
- 'melting'.

There may be some argument as to whether the words describing ice are relevant, but the main point to be made concerns text coherence. Without wanting to get deeply into the idea of 'lexical fields', it is worth drawing out the point about how a paragraph focuses on one idea or part of a story, and that a quick scan of vocabulary shows the focus of the passage.

Activity 4 Students sometimes find it difficult to appreciate that there is anything in their lives worth writing about, so the point that needs to be made for this activity is a variation of the 'write a lot about a little' advice which is often given to higher-ability GCSE students. Their challenge should be to make the fairly mundane engaging for a reader by the quality of the writing. The writing should be very concise, using the original passage as a model; it might be a good idea to impose a limit of, say, six sentences.

Using flashbacks

Write and assess activity: Organising events in a story

This section talks about using narrative devices to add interest. The use of flashback is one obvious way for students to 'craft' a text. A straightforward chronological narrative will often begin on a low key and lead up to some crisis or conflict that needs to be resolved. A writer could choose to begin on an extreme high point and then keep a reader in suspense by having a flashback which explores the events leading up to the opening scene, before ending with a resolution of the dramatic moment. The decision to tell the story in this way would provide evidence of a writer crafting a response rather than simply telling it as it happened.

Activity 5

a The change of tense comes towards the end of the passage: 'Coming downstairs after finding his torch, he overheard his mother say what she thought of the expedition.'

The point to be drawn out is that the change of tense is used to shape the structure of the story: the move from present to past introduces a flashback, a story that is not told chronologically. There could be discussion of why anyone would choose to tell a story non-chronologically. For example, there could be discussion of how a story about a death would be different if the story began with the death and then went into the past to explain the events leading up to it, rather than a story ending with the death of a character.

b The new character is the mother, after the focus has been on the father.

c The positive tone, the boy's admiration for his father, is replaced by the more negative, irritated tone introduced by the mother.

Activity 6 This activity is intended as practice for students rather than as an approach to a controlled assessment piece, but it could be either. To avoid this exercise taking up too much time, it might be a good strategy to share some ideas for plots with the class, or invite them all to attempt the suggestion in the book. The writing should be concise: the 'event' of the opening need be no more than someone crying or someone writing a message on a computer – it may be best to avoid over-dramatic openings, which might lead to over-long pieces of writing. The focus is on using the idea of flashback structure and some of the vivid detail practised in the previous task.

Introducing a 'twist'

This section introduces another variation of narrative structure that would need to be 'crafted'.

Activity 7 It would be best if the story was read aloud by the teacher, who could emphasise some of the stylistic features – particularly the way the writer shapes dialogue – that are going to be explored by the class.

a The simple answer to be drawn out is the use of single-word utterances that are given to the husband – a simple device to introduce contrast, as well as being a subtle hint about the way the story will unfold.

b There may be a variety of responses to this. The purpose of the question is to tease out that the repetition could be considered clumsy in the portrayal of speech – we might not want students to adopt it as a model for writing dialogue – but there is some underlying reason. One answer is that the constant repetition of 'Mr Decker' somehow emphasises the gap between the husband and wife. Perhaps by repeating 'Mr Decker' rather than 'Mrs Decker', the writer is hinting at the character who will emerge on top at the end of the story.

Activity 8 This, again, is writing practice rather than a controlled assessment piece, but depending on the controlled assessment tasks in any one year, the idea of a story with a satisfying twist may be relevant. The point to be emphasised to students is that a story with a twist has evidence of a writer explicitly thinking in interesting ways about structure, and structure is an assessment focus. As with other pieces of writing in this chapter, the aim should be to produce a concise piece of writing – the original is a very spare, brief piece of writing.

This would present a very good opportunity for peer assessment. Peer assessors could be invited to comment on:

- how interestingly the setting is described
- how effectively dialogue is used
- how good the 'twist' was: Could they see it coming? Were there any subtle hints that it was coming?

Stretch yourself

Connecting comments activity: Assessing creative writing

Another approach to writing non-fiction is to base a story on a photograph or image. This idea is developed further on Worksheet 19a.

The suggested activity is to write a poem. It will be important for students to understand that the structure they are using is:

- a setting in which a metaphor is established – in this case, 'light'
- an ending in which the significance of the setting is drawn out.

The potential metaphorical significance of light could be discussed with the class, but it should be fairly easy for higher-tier students to grasp the various possibilities.

It would also be possible to take the structure of the poem 'First Ice' and convert it into a piece of prose writing – the poem can easily become the basis of a story with flashback structure:

- a cold setting with an unhappy protagonist
- a flashback scene in which the reader finds out what led up to this
- an ending that returns to the time of the opening paragraph.

Outcomes

In this chapter your students have:

- explored different kinds of planning
- explored different ways of structuring their fiction writing.

20 Meeting the needs of your readers

AO focus

English AO3 Writing and English Language AO4 Writing.

- Write [to communicate] clearly, effectively and imaginatively, using and adapting forms and selecting vocabulary appropriate to task and purpose in ways that engage the reader.

In this chapter your students will:

- think about different ways of engaging their audience
- use a range of language features to suit audience and purpose.

Additional resources

Worksheets

20a: Thinking about purpose
20b: Influencing your readers
20c: Adding details to interest your readers 1
20d: Adding details to interest your readers 2

Getting started

As a starter activity you could ask students in groups or with a partner to make a list of all the purposes for writing that they can think of within a specified time limit – 5 minutes should suffice.

Purposes they are likely to cover are:

- inform
- explain
- advise
- instruct
- argue
- persuade
- describe.

This could be followed by asking students to give examples of texts for each of the identified purposes.

As an alternative starter you could give students a selection of texts and ask them to identify the purpose of each text, explaining the reasons for their choice. These could include:

- advertisements
- information leaflets
- sports reports
- articles
- advice columns
- instructions.

The supplements of Sunday newspapers are a useful source of texts written for a range of purposes.

At the end of the starter activities you may wish to ask students how easy or difficult it was for them to decide on the purpose of a text. Students who found this difficult will need to be given more guidance prior to tackling Activity 1.

Working through the chapter

The activities in this chapter reinforce for students how they must have audience and purpose in mind before they plan and write a text. The activities also help students to understand that often texts can have more than one purpose: for example, travel writing can both inform and describe. This notion may have become apparent to students during the starter activity, where there may have been some differences in the purposes assigned to texts.

Thinking about purpose

Activity 1 (Worksheet 20a) The aim of this activity is to establish the understanding that texts rarely have one purpose only. You may find it useful to give students some guidelines on how to identify the purpose of a text. They could use the following as a checklist.

- Type of vocabulary used, for example:
  - lots of adjectives
  - technical vocabulary
  - language used emotively.
- Type of sentences, for example:
  - directives
  - questions.
- Tone of the text, for example:
  - formal or informal
  - friendly or impersonal.

79

English and English Language Teacher's Book Higher Tier
Section B: Writing

Likely responses are as follows:

Text	Purpose 1	Evidence	Purpose 2	Evidence
A	Inform	… beef from the cattle … of Inner Mongolia.	Describe	… sit beautifully on an equally beautiful bone-china plate … fresh coriander …
B	Persuade	Use of positive language, such as 'self-confidence', 'hero', 'strength'.	Inform	Prices and types of aftershave products available.
C	Inform	… essential to enable our bodies … Casual exposure …	Advise	… before you strip off …

After completing this activity you may wish to generate some class discussion on the features and language style of each of the identified purposes. For example in Text B, the connotations of the vocabulary and the impact on the reader could be explored in further detail.

A follow-on activity could be to ask students to write their own advertisement in the same style, perhaps as a homework task.

Engaging the interest of your readers

Learning activity: Vocabulary and audience

The focus of this section is on how writers use language effectively and imaginatively. Before beginning Activity 2 you could ask students to write two or three lines on what they understand of the term 'using language effectively and imaginatively'. If their responses are written on post-it notes, they can be displayed for further reference as students produce their own writing.

Activity 2

a The purpose of this activity is to enable students to identify some the features of writing to describe. In this text they are:

- choice of adjectives and verbs
- appeal to the senses
- use of metaphor.

Likely responses are:

- Adjectives: good, freshly caught, beautiful, fresh, toasted, mouth-watering.
- Senses: sight, hearing, smell, taste.
- The metaphor 'a symphony of chopping …' conveys the sounds of the meal being prepared. The word 'symphony' suggests organisation and coordinated activity in the kitchen.
- Verbs: chopping, chatting, clattering. The effect of the three verbs together is to convey the hectic atmosphere in the kitchen.

b As students are asked to write a short paragraph (5–8 lines) this is a good opportunity for them to practise the skill of crafting their work, revising and rethinking to produce their very best writing.

Before they begin this task, you may wish to remind students that the overuse of adjectives, similes and metaphors does not lead to good writing. It is better to choose words carefully and sparingly, considering their effect on the reader. You could provide students with a thesaurus to enable them to make precise vocabulary choices.

Peer assessment provides a good opportunity for students to test out their writing on another reader. Once the first draft is written they could pass their work to a partner, who could use the bullet points as a checklist to assess the effectiveness of the writing and suggest alternative vocabulary where appropriate. After this, students will produce the final draft.

Maintaining the interest of your readers

The aim of this section is to encourage students to focus on how the writer maintains the interest of the reader throughout the structure of the text. The skills of identifying text cohesion and linking between paragraphs practised in Chapter 15 could be revisited here.

Activity 3
Likely answers could be as follows, though any valid answers based on the text are acceptable:

a The purpose of the comparison with London buses is to introduce readers to the idea that there are a lot of dinosaurs in the show. Readers may also be a little mystified by the comparison, which will encourage them to read on in the text.

b The comparison of the torosaurus with a Transit van enables readers to relate the size of the creature to something familiar – another way of engaging their interest.

c The reader's interest is engaged by the reference to 'a vicious-looking blighter'.

As further details about the creature are withheld until the following paragraph, this encourages the reader to read on, thus maintaining their interest.

d Making the dinosaurs sound interesting before revealing details about the Walking with Dinosaurs exhibition makes the reader want to read on to find out where they can go and see it.

e The writer appears to be fascinated by the creatures – students may quote details from paragraphs 2 and 3. He also seems a little frightened – 'a vicious-looking blighter' – and is in awe of them – 'Cor'. He may also feel drawn to them because they remind him of experiences from his childhood.

f The writer makes the dinosaurs seem like living creatures by referring to features such as 'long elegant neck', 'green eyes', 'stained teeth'. Other examples can be found in paragraph 3.

g Students should be encouraged to find two or three reasons to support their answer, whether it is in the affirmative or the negative.

Activity 4 Here students can practise what they have just learned about structure. You could point out that interesting writing begins with the choice of title: something they should bear in mind when writing their own piece.

Students should begin by preparing a plan based on the bullet points, and discussing it with another student to explain exactly how they intend to capture the interest of their readers.

Once the first draft is completed, students could exchange their work with the same partner for advice on improvements before writing the final draft. The bullet points should be used as criteria for this peer assessment.

Influencing your readers

Learning activity: Influencing your readers

Analysis activity: Tourism texts

You could ask students to read the article with a partner and to work out the purposes of the text before focusing on the activities that follow.

Activity 5 (Worksheet 20b) It may be helpful to copy Text E for students so that they can highlight relevant sections when completing the table.

a Likely responses are as given in the table at the bottom of the page.

b The first point to establish here is how to identify the target audience. Students should look at the content, vocabulary and tone to do this. It should be straightforward for them to identify the audience as teenage girls.

For this response, students should draw on their work on the features in part (a). They should provide evidence and explanation to justify their opinions on whether or not the tone is successful in appealing to the audience.

Activity 6 The focus of this activity is to enable students to match the tone of their writing to a specific audience. Once the first draft is written, students could annotate their own work using the bullet points. They could then show their work to another student, explaining the choices they have made.

The final test of success for their piece is whether it has persuaded another student.

Adding details to interest your readers

Correcting comments activity: Detail and description

Before reading Text F you could ask students to make notes in response to a series of questions about the behaviour and appearance of one of their own relatives at a family occasion. This may be helpful to those students who have difficulty adding detail to their writing.

Technique	Examples of usage	Effects
Use of personal pronouns, e.g. 'we', 'our', 'us', 'you'	We're turning down every invite …	Makes readers feel the writer shares their experiences/knows something about their lives
Use of words and phrases from reader's every day speech	… the animal known as party … it's still seriously Baltic	Engages readers by making them feel reading the text is like chatting with a friend
Humorous examples	… we don't have the advantage of make-up to tone down our embarrassingly red noses and cheeks	Entertains readers and helps them to relate to the text
Short sentences at key points in the text	It must be January. See you in February, girls.	Reinforces for readers the main point of the text

81

Suggested questions are:

- Does your relative have a loud or a quiet voice?
- How do they laugh?
- What do they wear when dressed up in a best outfit?
- Are they lively and confident or shy and self-effacing?
- How do they move around the room?
- How do they sit?

Activity 7 A copy is provided on Worksheet 20c, which you may wish to direct students to highlight as they complete the activities. Alternatively, this would make a good whole-class activity, with the text displayed on an interactive whiteboard.

a It could be helpful to students to work out the balance between description of appearance and actions to help them realise that a focus on actions can be a useful way of building up detail in a description.

Likely responses to (b) to (e) are:

b The uncles' actions – for example, 'holding out their cigars at arm's length' – suggest they are not experienced smokers, possibly trying to show off with their cigars.

c The aunts' actions – sitting on 'the very edges of their chairs' – suggest they are rather nervous ladies, ill-at-ease and probably unused to being out in company.

d The first simile – 'as though waiting for the explosion' – reinforces the uncles' lack of experience, adds a comic air to the description.

The second simile – 'like faded cups and saucers' – reinforces the self-effacing nature of the aunts, as well as emphasising their age in the use of the word 'faded'.

e The commas help to build the description by allowing the writer to include a range of interesting details in one sentence. The commas also enable the writer to make asides, as in 'nor anywhere else for that matter'.

You may also wish to use the semi-colon in the paragraph as a teaching point.

Activity 8 The short length of the task should encourage students to craft their writing carefully.

They may wish to produce several drafts before they are satisfied that they have produced a good description. Peer and self-assessment throughout the stages of writing, using the bullet points as criteria, will enable students to improve their work.

Stretch yourself

These are intended as extension activities for more able students, who should be able to access the text and the activities alone or in pairs. A copy of the text is provided on Worksheet 20d. There is also potential for displaying the text on a whiteboard, where the structure and the details used to build description can be highlighted for whole-class discussion.

1 Structure of the text

- Paragraph 1: information given about Mrs Joe, with reference to Joe Gargery in the final sentence.
- Paragraph 2: describes the appearance and character of Joe, with reference to his relationship with Mrs Joe.
- Paragraph 3: includes more details of the appearance and character of Mrs Joe, together with the narrator's opinion of her.

Details used to build up description

Students should be encouraged to select their own examples.

2 It is advisable for students to plan this activity before writing, in order to explore/consider a range of suitable vocabulary and techniques.

As in previous activities, working with a partner at both the planning and drafting stages can assist in the production of high-quality writing.

Outcomes

In this chapter your students have:

- examined the audience and purpose of a range of texts
- examined the way writers use language and purpose to engage their readers
- used language in an interesting way to engage their readers
- selected details to make their writing interesting.

21 Different kinds of writing

AO focus

English AO3 Writing and English Language AO4 Writing.

- Write [to communicate] clearly, effectively and imaginatively, using and adapting forms and selecting vocabulary appropriate to task and purpose in ways that engage the reader.

In this chapter your students will:

- practise writing a variety of kinds of imaginative writing
- explore and experiment with aspects of different genres.

Additional resources

Worksheets

21a: Exploring genres

21b: Satire

Getting started

There are two main focuses in this chapter. One focus is on different genres of prose and prose fiction, and the other is on the differences between drama, poetry and prose – AO3 establishes that students need to be confident in 'using and adapting forms'.

The controlled assessment tasks in GCSE English, 'producing creative texts', do not always specify the form or genre of writing, so students may choose to write poetry or drama script. It could be important, therefore, to allow them opportunities to practise these different forms. If they choose to write prose stories, they will be helped by considering different aspects of the genre in which they choose to write.

It would be a good idea to invite students to compile lists of the various genres they know. They could be started off with horror and romance, before compiling longer lists. When they have a list it would also be a good idea to see if they are aware of subgenres. The easiest way to approach this may be to focus on films. There could be discussion of what genres films belong to, a discussion that might show that some films could belong to more than one genre. They could be asked, for example, what genre of film *Harry Potter* belongs to; this might lead to discussion of the notion of an 'adventure' genre.

It would also be useful to explore the genres of television programmes. Students could list the various genres and exemplify them.

Working through the chapter

Genres

k! Learning activity: Genre

As students may have started their approach to this chapter by listing genres and subgenres, it would be a good idea to explore genres further by looking at the conventions of particular genres. Different students or groups of students could be given the task of listing the conventions of various genres, such as horror, science fiction, adventure, spy, thriller, romcom. It would be helpful for groups to produce a display that exemplifies books/films/programmes which belong to a genre and lists the conventions that characterise it.

Description

k! Write and assess activity: Descriptive writing

An additional extract, from *Jane Eyre,* is provided on Worksheet 21a. This can be used alongside the three texts given in the Student Book for Activities 1–5.

Activity 1

- Students may suggest fantasy, historical, possibly horror. The main issue is that they identify particular features of the writing, such as the old-fashioned vocabulary and the strange, slightly sinister imagery.
- Describing the candelabrum as a 'spider'; the drawer half-open and full of something as strange as birdseed; the growing mound of candle wax.
- It makes it sound almost threatening, giving the room a sinister atmosphere – spiders trap things in webs.
- The alternatives would lighten the atmosphere and remove the slightly threatening mood.

Activity 2

k! Learning activity: Vocabulary and genre

- Most students will identify this as some kind of travel writing, something like a tourist guide.
- The 'cobwebs' are easy to 'clear away', so lack the threat of the spider in the first passage. They are also surrounded by more positive features of the scene: 'stroll ... green ... pretty'. The description mentions lots of people and 'ordinary' activities – cycling,

83

English and English Language Teacher's Book Higher Tier
Section B: Writing

walking – in public spaces. The only feature of the scene that could be seen as 'horror' might be 'woods', which have certain connotations, but the surrounding details are completely positive. References to 'hordes of' people lack the focus on isolated individuals that you get in horror.

- An example might be: 'On the other side of the dark Gare de Lyon, where the old wine market once stood, he found himself, alone, in the parc de Bercy where the trees of the orchard closed around him.'

Activity 3

- Use of 'griping' suggests the smog is not to be taken too seriously – the fault seems to lie with the people rather than the smog. The list of examples of harmful effects of the pollution seems not to be entirely serious ('if the Pekinese had fleas').
- This narrator, like the narrator in Text A, begins with a focus on something unpleasant, but, unlike the previous narrator, this one pokes fun at the unpleasantness and ends on an upbeat note rather than downbeat.

Activity 4

a Text A is from the Gothic fantasy, *Titus Groan*; Text B is from a Lonely Planet travel guide; and Text C is from the crime story *The Long Goodbye*.

b Text B focuses on places, gives information, uses the second person to directly address the reader. In this instance, the text also assumes a quite educated, probably middle-class readership.

Text C uses a first-person narrator and creates a wise-cracking, slightly cynical character. The vocabulary is fairly colloquial.

Activity 5 Student rewrites should be shared and writers invited to draw attention explicitly to the features of language they have adapted.

Activity 6 'Ordinary' features are made to seem threatening by:

- **the choice of vocabulary**: 'sluggish', 'black', 'unpleasantly', 'clammy', 'damp', 'stale', 'hating', 'hostile', 'terrified', 'hidden', 'whip', 'unattractive', 'cold', 'hostile'.
- **the introduction of uncertainty**: for example, as the eyes of the portrait seem to be watching the protagonist.

Activity 7 Students should reflect on the previous activities, in which they have explored, briefly, some features of travel writing and Gothic/horror/

ghost writing. Ideas about the photograph could be shared on the board, for example:

- Were this photograph to be part of a travel brochure, what would the accompanying text be?
- What features of this photograph could be used to create a sinister atmosphere?

Each paragraph should only contain a few sentences – five or six would suffice.

A different form

Drama

Learning activity: Drama

Students will be used to reading plays, but may not have spent very much time considering the practical or technical considerations of drama. The following activities are intended to focus students on some of the challenges of writing a drama text.

Activity 8

a The answers are:

- all the details about the river
- any mention of the mountains
- the detailed descriptions of the trees
- the animals that are not actually there when the characters appear but we are told are a feature of the area
- the information about the nature of the path
- the rabbits and the heron which leave the scene.

b Reasons could include:

- because of the impracticality of it
- the impossibility of having a river on stage
- the improbability of having animals, especially birds, on stage.

c The rabbits were removed because of the impossibility of having them on stage, and the heron is also obviously impractical.

It would be worthwhile spending some time discussing the limitations of stage and how dramatists overcome them. The central issue is how the two forms – drama and fiction – work in different ways.

Activity 9 It would be possible to write the script for a radio version of the opening of *Of Mice and Men*. The challenges would include:

- **How to establish the names of the places**: it could only be achieved by the use of a narrator

84

in the drama, or by inventing some dialogue between the two central characters in which the places were named (it could be worthwhile asking students to see if this can be done effectively).

- **How to convey the beauty of the scene**: sound effects could capture running water, but not its colour or warmth.
- **How to establish the basic geography of the scene**: things like the path.

The point to be established is how prose allows writers to achieve effects which present difficult challenges for those writing for the stage. Students could also consider how film as a form creates possibilities that are not open to the stage dramatist.

Activity 10 The focus here should be on creating a picture of a place and establishing a tone for a listener. Students should consider a mix of words and sound effects. For example, a countryside or city-centre setting could be established with clever use of sound effects, so that words could be used to describe interesting detail.

If sound effects of birds singing and cows mooing are played, there is no need for the narrator to say the birds were singing and there were cows in the field.

Poetry
Learning activity: Poetry

In their controlled assessment, students are probably more likely to write poetry as an alternative to prose, rather than drama script; it is easier to see how poetry will allow students to meet assessment criteria concerning structure and vocabulary choices.

Activity 11

a   There are various patterns:
- the repetition of 'She pops home just long enough'
- the repetition of 'to' followed by a verb
- the decreasing pattern of lines in each stanza: 6, 5, 4, etc.

b   That she is a bit of an irritation.

c   It suggests she brings light and life and vitality to their lives.

d   There could be various answers to this: some readers might think the last line suggests the parents could not cope with much more of their daughter; others might think that the last line is left for the reader to fill in their own response – just long enough for what? The poem ends up being about the parents rather than the daughter.

Activity 12 The link needs to be established with the original Cal Clothier poem: how the idea of the poem shifts subtly.

The poem could be based on a real person, a real relationship, but it does not have to be: students could explore ideas about relationships by imagining a person.

Stretch yourself
While there is no extension activity in the Student Book, a possible task is provided on Worksheet 21b.

Outcomes

In this chapter your students have:
- explored some different genres of writing
- experimented with different kinds of writing.

22 Making your writing skills count in the exam

AO focus

English AO3 Writing and English Language AO4 Writing.

- Write [to communicate] clearly, effectively and imaginatively, using and adapting forms and selecting vocabulary appropriate to task and purpose in ways that engage the reader.
- Organise information and ideas into structured and sequenced sentences, paragraphs and whole texts, using a variety of linguistic and structural features to support cohesion and overall coherence.
- Use a range of sentence structures for clarity, purpose and effect, with accurate punctuation and spelling.

In this chapter your students will:

- learn more about how their writing is tested in the exam
- study questions in a sample paper
- plan, write and assess an answer
- read other students' answers and the examiner's comments on them.

Working through the chapter

About the exam

This section makes clear what students have to do in their GCSE English or GCSE English Language exam. It is worth stressing the significant number of marks that students can gain by doing well in this.

What you need to know

The Assessment Objectives are written for teachers, not students. This section of the Student Book breaks down the Assessment Objectives and explains them in ways that have meaning for the students. It is important that students are helped to internalise these; to do this, they need to be helped to access the language. You may want to do a quick check on their understanding of the terminology. A useful task is to ask them to rewrite the Assessment Objectives in a way that would be understood by Year 9 students. They can develop points and use examples to illustrate them in whatever way they choose. As a class, you could discuss the terminology they had most difficulty in explaining or simplifying, and explore the reasons for this.

Students should be made aware that all these skills have been covered in the Writing chapters in the Student Book.

Sample questions

- Planning activity: The Writing exam 1
- Connecting comments activity: The Writing exam 2
- On your marks activity: The Writing exam 3

The questions in the exam are based on the Assessment Objectives. The two questions given in the Student Book are typical of those set for this paper. Emphasise that the first question is worth fewer marks than the second. Students only have 1 hour in which to plan and write answers to two writing tasks. They need to balance their time carefully. As a simple guide, they could allow 25 minutes for the first task and 35 minutes for the second task.

Steps A–E in the Student Book exemplify what students need to do before writing, using Question 1. This stage is often neglected, especially when time is limited. Students need to be helped to understand that a few minutes purposefully planning makes a measurable difference to their final piece of writing. It is a good idea to regularly spend time on the development of the different stages of planning techniques throughout their GCSE course.

Here are a few ideas to help you do this:

Step A: A common complaint of examiners is that students do not answer the given question. Your aim is to ensure that students read the question carefully and know exactly what they have to do. You could give them five questions such as those listed below. For each one they have to identify the subject, purpose, audience and form.

- Write an article for a magazine in which you explain to your readers why you are interested in a particular sport or hobby.
- You have recently read an article in a local newspaper which suggests that people under the age of 18 should not be allowed to use internet chatrooms. Write a letter to the newspaper in which you argue for or against this view.
- Imagine that have recently done work experience in a large department store. Write an article for your school website in which you inform your readers about your experience.

86

- Write a letter to an elderly relative explaining why you hope he or she will be able to spend Christmas with you and your family.
- You have been asked to make a presentation to the governors of your school, informing them of the ways in which the school environment could be improved. Write the text for the speech you would make.

Step B: Students often run out of things to say in the middle of their writing. They then either finish early or move on to a separate subject. They need help in gathering ideas before they write.

Students who lack confidence in their own ideas can often be helped by working in pairs or small groups. You could take two of the above tasks and ask students to gather as many relevant ideas as they can.

A useful tip for students struggling to gather ideas is to give prompts in the form of the questions: Who? What? Where? When? How? Why? Make it clear that, at this stage, they are making no commitment to write about them.

You could then collate the ideas on the board and discuss the range and suitability of these. Keep a copy of these ideas for use when you come to do some work on Step C.

Step C: This is the stage of planning where the student takes control of their writing. They decide where to start, where to finish and how to get from one point to the other. The analogy with a journey often works well. You could display the ideas produced in previous planning activities and ask them to select from these and make a brief paragraph plan. Sometimes students simply write 'Introduction' beside their first paragraph and 'Conclusion' beside their final paragraph. This is of no real value and it helps to insist that they should make clear what detail their introduction and conclusion will contain.

Step D: Before writing, students need to go through a mental tick list of the skills they need to demonstrate in their writing. They need to:

- engage and interest their reader
- use Standard English
- use a range of sentence structures
- use a varied, mature vocabulary
- make sure their writing is technically accurate.

You could ask them to create a mnemonic to help them remember these. This is often more useful than having one provided for them. It forces them to think carefully about what they need to do and to come up with an idea that has specific personal significance. They could then share these with other students and could, if they wanted to, use a suggestion they prefer.

Step E: Many students simply repeat the question or part of it in their opening sentence. A useful tactic for helping them to avoid this is to ban the use of any of the significant words in the task. It is best to avoid confusion and write the question on the board with the banned words crossed out, for example:

> ~~Write~~ an ~~article~~ for a ~~magazine~~ in which you ~~explain~~ to your ~~readers~~ why you are ~~interested~~ in a ~~particular sport~~ or ~~hobby~~.

You could also encourage them to write a number of different potential opening sentences, using the following techniques:

- rhetorical questions
- short sentences
- descriptive writing
- exclamations.

They could then select their preferred option from these and discuss the reasons for their choice.

Activity 1 Students are asked to plan and write a response to Question 2 in 35 minutes. You may wish to allow longer for this task as they are learning how to do it. They will become quicker with practice. Encourage students to read through their own work carefully before sharing it with other students. You could distribute record sheets for students to record their comments on each other's work. They should keep these comments for later.

Sample answers

Students are given two sample answers to the question they have just answered. Each answer has been commented on by an examiner. Notice in Text A that the positive comments come first. You need to constantly reinforce the good things that students do in their writing so that they continue to do them, before pointing out how to progress. For example, Student A needs to be congratulated on the use of paragraphs and then helped to make paragraphing coherent and effective. If students are assessing each other's writing, it helps to insist that they list at least three positive comments and no more than two negative ones.

As an alternative approach to this section, you could photocopy the two responses without the examiner's comments and ask students to assess their qualities. It is worth noting that students are often more critical than examiners in the comments they make. Point out that most examiners are teachers who want the students to do well. They are looking to reward the positive qualities of the writing, and their final assessment reflects what the student has achieved rather than what they have failed to do. Once students have written their assessments, they can then compare them with those made by the examiner.

Students always want to know the grade. However, you may find it helpful to either withhold references to grades completely or keep any revelation until the end of a task. This helps to keep students focused on the qualities of the writing and what any given student needs to do to improve. If you want to reveal grades at the end of the task, then Student A is writing at a notional grade C level. Student B, for whom there are no negative comments, is writing at a notional grade A* level.

Activity 2 Students now have the opportunity to apply to their own writing what they have learned from the study of Text A and Text B. They should reconsider the comments made on their writing response and on the two students' writing, and list ways in which they could improve their answer. You could ask them to redraft it, but a more interesting challenge, which could be set as homework, would be to answer a fresh question, such as the one below:

- Write an article for a magazine read by people your age in which you argue for or against the idea that teenagers have a better life now than they have ever had.

If you wanted to, you could, with your students' permission, use a selection of these responses as the basis for further assessment.

Outcomes

In this chapter your students have:

- studied how the Assessment Objective for Writing is tested in the exam
- examined questions in a sample paper
- planned and written a sample answer
- studied sample answers and examiner's comments
- considered how to achieve the highest marks they can in their exam.

23 Making your writing skills count in the controlled assessment

AO focus

English AO3 Writing and English Language AO4 Writing.

- Write [to communicate] clearly, effectively and imaginatively, using and adapting forms and selecting vocabulary appropriate to task and purpose in ways that engage the reader.
- Organise information and ideas into structured and sequenced sentences, paragraphs and whole texts, using a variety of linguistic and structural features to support cohesion and overall coherence.
- Use a range of sentence structures for clarity, purpose and effect, with accurate punctuation and spelling.

In this chapter your students will:

- learn more about how their writing is assessed in controlled assessment
- learn more about the tasks in controlled assessment
- read other students' answers and the examiner's comments on them.

Additional resources

Worksheets

23a: Basing writing on a poem
23b: Important places

Working through the chapter

What is controlled assessment?

Once they begin the final stage of their controlled assessment, students will have no access to teacher feedback or to resources such as thesauruses, dictionaries or spell-checkers. This makes the preparation/planning stage of controlled assessment very important. Working through the chapters in the Student Book will help them in their general preparation for the controlled assessment before they focus on the precise task.

The Assessment Objectives are the same in the exam and controlled assessment, but in the latter students have far more time (up to 4 hours) to complete two tasks, whereas they only have 1 hour in the exam to complete a long and a short writing task.

In previous specifications it was quite common for students to complete creative writing tasks at an early stage of the course; in these specifications it would be best to spend more time preparing students and developing their skills.

Where every student in the class is being entered for the same specification, they can focus on the appropriate specification panel in the Student Book. If students are being entered for different specifications, it should be quite easy to see the many similarities – the same AOs are applicable.

There is one important distinction to be made:

- **GCSE English:** in this specification there is a little more focus on 'creative' or imaginative.
- **GCSE English Language:** in this specification there is a little more focus on non-fiction writing.

The category of 'Moving images' is common to both specifications. The kinds of writing required under that heading are different in the two specifications:

- **GCSE English:** students will be invited, for example, to create atmospheric settings in writing, having watched a film or television drama.
- **GCSE English Language:** students will be invited to produce things like film reviews or scripts for documentary voice-overs.

'Prompts and re-creations' is also a feature of both specifications and, like 'Moving images', requires different kinds of writing in each specification.

- **GCSE English:** this will involve students in converting one literary text into another.
- **GCSE English Language:** students will usually be invited to create a non-fiction text from the stimulus of a literary one, perhaps something like a journalistic response to a situation in a text.

It is worthwhile noting that the controlled assessment writing for both specifications can be linked to other aspects of the GCSE courses. The kinds of non-fiction writing required for GCSE English Language will be excellent preparation for the more tightly timed writing in the exam in Unit 1, and the imaginative re-creations in GCSE English should also help students in their study of literary texts, a feature of the reading section of the controlled assessment.

In both specifications students have to produce two pieces of writing, but there is no requirement for them to be produced very close to each other: the time allowed may be spread through the course. Arrangements will be different in different centres, but it would be a good idea to explain to students how the controlled assessment will be conducted in terms of:

- when it will take place
- whether the students will choose tasks or be directed by the centre
- how use of computers will be controlled.

It should be made clear to students that they are not allowed to write a complete response before the controlled assessment and seek feedback from their teacher, with a view to replicating something similar in controlled conditions.

Introducing the tasks

On your marks activity: The Writing controlled assessment 1

There are three options for the controlled assessment tasks.

GCSE English

- Moving images (writing for or about moving images)
- Prompts and re-creations (using a text or prompt to develop writing)
- Me. Myself. I. (writing from personal experience)

Students will produce two pieces of writing in response to tasks from two of these categories totalling around 1,600 words across both pieces.

GCSE English Language

- Moving images (writing for or about moving images)
- Commissions (responding to a given brief)
- Re-creations (taking a text and turning it into another)

Students will produce two pieces of writing in response to tasks from two of these categories, totalling around 1,200 words across both pieces.

In cases where the school is going to direct the students about which task they are going to undertake there will be no need to explore the different options at any length, but it would be a good idea to point out the level of choice that exists in each option.

It would be a good idea to remind students about the Assessment Objectives and about some of the work they have done in other chapters: the work was focused on different aspects of the AOs.

Sample questions and sample answers

Prompts and re-creations

Connecting comments activity: The Writing controlled assessment 2

Writing poetry for assessment is something that should not be undertaken lightly. The section on planning shows how important it is to plan to meet the Assessment Objectives: free verse, for example, could be very difficult to match to Assessment Objectives concerning structure. Use of a variety of punctuation is as important in poetry as in prose. The section on planning provides a kind of template – ideas, form and structure, use of language – which is intended to help focus candidates on assessment criteria.

The 'Teacher's comments' are also focused on Assessment Objectives.

Activity 1 (Worksheet 23a) This is a brief activity, the purpose of which is to get students thinking about an idea they want to develop from the poem. It does not require a detailed exploration of the quite demanding Blake poem to be able to undertake the task. A starting point could be exemplified: the city is full of sadness and corruption.

Moving images

Activity 2 This activity, because it is more creative than non-fiction, is more likely to be found in GCSE English than GCSE English Language.

a This could be the basis of some effective work for En1. Students could be invited to talk about particular scenes, either as part of a whole-class discussion or as a small group exercise. If time and equipment allowed, there could be presentations which use clips from DVDs.

b–c As students list and talk about scenes, the various atmospheres they are describing could be listed on the board. At this stage it would be most effective if some short clips could be watched. Black-and-white films might produce particularly effective discussion. One particularly important word to introduce is 'contrast'. It could also be important to look at *mise-en-scène*: discussion of the significance of objects and where they are placed could feed into a discussion of the importance of imagery in students' atmospheric writing.

Activity 3 Students should notice the way several sentences in Text D begin 'The …' and also that there is little evidence of in-sentence punctuation – the only use of the comma, for example, is in the punctuation of speech. Despite these potential signs of weakness, there is a lot to admire in the writing. The piece is carefully structured, opening with some scene-setting which also establishes a quite suspenseful atmosphere (although there may be discussion of the effectiveness of the image of the 'million little creatures').

This opening doesn't just focus on sight, it also describes sounds. The writing is then focused on the two children, and sparing dialogue is introduced with a great deal of control and skill. The sentences become shorter as the tension is ratcheted upwards. Student discussion of what the writer should improve should focus on the manipulation of sentence structures and punctuation for effect.

> *Me. Myself. I.* **[GCSE English only]**
> This is likely to be a popular choice in many centres; several schools already have units of work based on autobiographical writing. An example of a task from this topic area is provided on Worksheet 23b: Write about a place that has been important to you.
>
> The focus should be on students' interpretation of 'important'. Perhaps the main point to establish is that this process is about selection – that it is a good idea to consider various ideas before homing in on one.

Outcomes

Planning activity: The Writing controlled assessment 3

In this chapter your students have:

- learned about how their writing skills are tested in the controlled assessment
- learned more about the ways they can achieve high marks in this part of the course.

Section C: Speaking and listening

Overview

Section C of the Student Book is designed to develop students' skills in speaking and listening as defined by the Assessment Objectives for GCSE English (AO1 Speaking and listening) and GCSE English Language (AO1 Speaking and listening) and tested in the controlled assessments.

GCSE English: AO1 Speaking and listening
GCSE English Language: AO1 Speaking and listening

- Speak to communicate clearly and purposefully; structure and sustain talk, adapting it to different situations and audiences; use Standard English and a variety of techniques as appropriate.
- Listen and respond to speakers' ideas and perspectives, and how they construct and express their meanings.
- Interact with others, shaping meanings through suggestions, comments and questions and drawing ideas together.
- Create and sustain different roles.

The chapters provide opportunities for students to draw on and revise the skills they have already acquired in speaking and listening, and to develop these further. The learning objectives, founded in the Assessment Objectives but in 'student-friendly' language, are given at the start of each chapter. Throughout each chapter the learning points are clarified and modelled, and followed by activities that are designed to reinforce and extend students' learning.

Students are encouraged to work independently or in pairs or small groups, as appropriate, and are given regular opportunities to assess their personal progress and that of other students, often against fixed criteria. The learning within the chapters is cumulative, building on what has come before, and at the end of several chapters there is a summative activity that challenges students to demonstrate their learning across the whole section.

Each chapter can be used as a discrete stand-alone topic, with activities and tasks specific to the named objectives. The order in which they appear in the Student Book does not have to be followed, though it is worth noting that this order was arrived at after careful consideration of how best to build students' skills in speaking and listening.

Assessment

GCSE English and GCSE English Language
Controlled assessment: three equally weighted activities:
- Presenting (15 marks)
- Discussing and listening (15 marks)
- Role playing (15 marks).

Section C
Speaking and listening

Nelson Thornes resources

Chapter	Student Book activities	kerboodle! resources
24: Building skills in speaking and listening	1: Paired discussion as to what makes a good speaker, using images for stimulus 2: Prioritising speaking skills in order of importance 3: Preparing a short talk focusing on three speaking skills 4: Listening to an article being read aloud and then reporting back on it 5: Self-evaluating speaking and listening skills 6: Paired discussion offering advice to students who want to improve their speaking and listening skills Review and reflect: Setting personal targets for developing speaking and listening skills	• Analysis activity: Body language • Audio case study activity: Effective speaking • Learning activity: A good listener • Learning activity: Speaking and listening terminology
25: Presenting	1: Identifying key features of good and bad presentations 2: Identifying examples of non-Standard English 3: Suggesting examples from students' own language that are non-Standard English 4: Assessing whether Standard English should be used in a range of example presentations 5: Improvising possible ways of opening a presentation and deciding which is most effective 6: Noting key points to include in a presentation; receiving feedback from a partner on the key points 7: Identifying examples of good/bad body language in presentations 8: Preparing a short presentation to be given to the rest of the class Stretch yourself: Preparing and delivering a presentation to the rest of the class	• Learning activity: A changing language • Video case study activity: Presentations • Analysis activity: Studying speeches • Learning activity: A news presentation • Worksheet 25a: Presentations: openings • Worksheet 25b: PowerPoint • Worksheet 25c: Speeches
26: Discussing and listening	1: Prioritising listening skills in order of importance 2: Reporting back on a partner's talk 3: Identifying useful questions to ask during a discussion 4: Practising asking questions to help the speaker develop their points 5: Paired discussion based around selecting a charity for the year group to support Review and reflect: Assessing performance in the paired discussion task 6: Group discussion and preparing a report about activities for a Year 7 events week Review and reflect: Discussing good and bad points about the group interaction in Activity 6	• Learning activity: Question types • Video case study activity: An interview • Learning activity: Group roles • Analysis activity: Transcript analysis

English and English Language Teacher's Book Higher Tier
Section C: Speaking and listening

Chapter	Student Book activities	kerboodle! resources
27: Creating and sustaining roles	1: Experimenting with tone of voice using single words 2: Improvising a telephone call using single words and practising tone of voice 3: Experimenting with tone and emphasis using short phrases 4: Practising using body language to convey meaning 5: Analysing body language in images; experimenting with body language to create a range of characters 6: Using a range of vocabulary to convey different phrases; selecting vocabulary to suit a particular character 7: Delivering and assessing a role play based around an interview 8: Delivering and assessing a role play as part of a small group 9–10: Developing a role play based on a character from a text	• Analysis activity: Finding characters • Case study activity: Characters of the imagination • Audio role-play activity: In the hotseat
28: Making your speaking and listening skills count in the controlled assessment	1: Comparing student responses to a 'Presenting' task and deciding which is the better response 2: Comparing student responses to a 'Discussing and listening' task and deciding which is the better response 3: Comparing student responses to a 'Role-playing' task and deciding which is the better response 4: Test knowledge of key words and phrases	• Planning activity: The Speaking and listening controlled assessment 1 • Connecting comments activity: The Speaking and listening controlled assessment 2 • On your marks activity: The Speaking and listening controlled assessment 3 • Worksheet 28a: Key words

Section C
Speaking and listening

Student checklist worksheet

Use the questions below to assess your speaking and listening skills and to set your personal speaking and listening targets.

Skill	Very confident	Quite confident	Sometimes I can	Often I can't	Which chapters might help?
Speak clearly to communicate my ideas and views					24
Use Standard English in my speech when appropriate					25
Structure my presentations effectively					25
Contribute to a discussion by asking questions, making suggestions and comments and drawing ideas together					26
Listen to the views of others, ask questions about and make comments on these					26
Take on and sustain different roles					27
Use voice, vocabulary and gesture to develop roles					27

Use your responses to the checklist to set yourself *no more than* three targets to achieve from the Speaking and listening section.

1. ....

2. ....

3. ....

95

English and English Language Teacher's Book Higher Tier
Section C: Speaking and listening

Checking students' progress

The tasks below are all included in the Student Book and can be used to check student progress in a particular skill.

Chapters	AO focus	Activities from Student Book and learning outcomes
25	• Speak to communicate clearly and purposefully; structure and sustain talk; use Standard English and a variety of techniques as appropriate.	**Chapter 25, Stretch yourself** Students: • prepare and deliver a talk to the rest of the class on a topic they feel strongly about • plan their talk beforehand • use appropriate techniques to structure their talk and engage their listeners.
26	• Interact with others, shaping meanings through suggestions, comments and questions and drawing ideas together.	**Chapter 26, Activity 6a** Students: • contribute to a group discussion • introduce new ideas to move the discussion forward • ask questions to help others review their points • listen to the ideas of others • refer to others' ideas in the points they make.
27	• Create and sustain different roles.	**Chapter 27, Activity 8** Students: • take part in a role play based on a domestic situation of their own devising • include between two and four characters • use a range of techniques to develop their character through voice, vocabulary, gesture, expression and mood.

General resources

The resources in the Student Book, Teacher's Book and *kerboodle!* provide a range of learning opportunities for students and give them practice at developing their skills using a wide variety of text types. In addition, examples of speeches can be found on many websites (for example, go to www.guardian.co.uk and search for 'Great speeches'). These can be used to reinforce, develop and extend students' skills and learning further.

24 Building skills in speaking and listening

AO focus

English AO1 Speaking and listening and English Language AO3 Speaking and listening.

- Speak to communicate clearly and purposefully.
- Listen and respond to speakers' ideas.

In this chapter your students will:

- think about the skills needed to be a good speaker and listener
- practise some of these skills
- evaluate their performance in speaking and listening tasks.

Getting started

As an introduction to Speaking and listening at Key Stage 4, you could begin by asking students to work with a partner to reflect on Speaking and listening activities they have enjoyed at Key Stage 3. These could include activities where they have been observing other students.

They could each write down three activities they have enjoyed, with a short explanation giving reasons to justify their choices.

As a continuation of the above, you could give each student a post-it note and ask them to write down three things they think make a good speaker and listener. The post-it notes could then be displayed on a speaking and listening noticeboard and used for whole-class reference. They could be added to as students develop greater skills and understanding as they work through the activities.

Working through the chapter

Throughout the chapter students will build on the skills and knowledge about speaking and listening that they have acquired throughout Key Stage 3. They will be encouraged to work with increasing independence, reflecting on their own performances and those of others.

Many of them will be confident speakers in a range of situations, such as role play, debates, giving presentations and taking part in group discussions, whereas others may not be so confident and experienced.

Some students entering Key Stage 4 may have difficulty participating in constructive group work, while for others this will present no problem. Some students may be uncomfortable with role play and as a result may exhibit inappropriate behaviour. It is likely that your students will cover a range of abilities in speaking and listening, and that considerable skill will have to be exercised to ensure that they all perform to their potential.

What makes a good speaker?

k! Analysis activity: Body language

k! Audio case study activity: Effective speaking

Students will have identified their own ideas about what makes a good speaker and listener in the starter activity. This could be continued by asking them to work in groups to come up with three or four reasons why it is important to become an accomplished speaker and listener.

Some of the reasons they might come up with include:

- Good speaking and listening skills can help you in job interviews.
- Becoming a good speaker and listener can increase your confidence and can help you to take a more active part in lessons.
- Many jobs require people to work as part of a team sharing ideas, so clearly good speaking and listening skills are important here.
- If you are asked to give a presentation at your sports club or other out-of-school activity, you will feel confident and able to tackle this.

Activity 1 The image stimulus provides an opportunity for students to reflect on the ways in which facial expression and body language can contribute to oral communication.

Some of their comments may include:

- good speakers look confidently at the audience
- body language is used to emphasise their words
- their body language makes them look confident.

Some explanations for not-so-good speakers may include:

- they do not maintain eye contact
- their body language indicates they are nervous and are not likely to speak well as a result.

Activity 2 Before starting this activity it would be useful to discuss the statements with the students to ensure their complete understanding of them.

97

Students could work in small groups or with a partner to identify one or two situations to match each statement. For instance, for 'varies vocabulary to suit audience', some example situations could be:

- a teacher telling a story to small children would use simple vocabulary
- in a job interview a student would use polite formal vocabulary.

There is no hierarchy for the skills on the list; all are important. However, the task of identifying an order enables students to reflect on what is required to be a good speaker at Key Stage 4. You could also ask them to justify the order they have chosen.

Activity 3 A short time – 15 minutes or so – should be allowed to prepare for and practise the task. This could be set as homework. Peer assessment could be used when students deliver their talk to a partner or a small group, using the checklist to make their judgements and to feed back suggestions for improvement to their partners.

Students could be invited to nominate very good speakers to perform their 60-second talks for the rest of the class.

Learning to be a good listener

As a teacher you will already be prepared for the very wide range of listening skills among students in your classes, which can sometimes be linked to levels of concentration. A useful starter could be to ask students to sit in silence for 60 seconds and to note down all the sounds they can hear. This has the dual purpose of aiding concentration and drawing attention to how much students can hear if they really listen.

This could be followed by asking students to write on post-it notes three reasons why listening is important. Their reasons need not be linked to school situations, allowing them to see the importance of listening in their lives as a whole.

Some likely responses are as follows:

- You learn better if you are a good listener.
- You will get on better with your friends if you listen carefully when they are telling you a story or about the difficulties in their lives.
- In work situations, when people are telling you about health and safety rules, it is very important to listen carefully.
- In a discussion you need to listen carefully to the ideas of others so that you can make your own points appropriately.

Activity 4

Learning activity: A good listener

Before starting this activity you may wish to revise/reintroduce listening skills to the whole class by playing a recording of news items and asking students to identify the main points.

When reading the text, students should be advised to read slowly and clearly so that their partners can follow the ideas more easily. Repeat readings can be allowed.

Evaluating your skills

Self-evaluation is an important aid to student progress, particularly in the area of speaking and listening where evidence is usually ephemeral. Reflecting on their targets and achievements after taking part in Speaking and listening tasks will help them to improve on their next performance.

Part of the preparation for the controlled tasks could be the production of a Speaking and listening portfolio, in which students record their targets and reflections after a range of tasks. Their responses to the quiz in Activity 5 could be the first item in the portfolio.

Activity 5 The questions in the quiz are based on the Speaking and listening criteria in the AQA specification. The purpose of this activity is to enable students to give an honest assessment of their current abilities and to give them a clear idea of targets for improvement.

Many students enjoy quizzes and are sometimes tempted to tick boxes indiscriminately. It should be stressed that they should think carefully about each choice and give truthful answers.

Once students have added up their scores they could comment on the feedback with a partner. Comments could include whether each student has given an accurate assessment of their own abilities (some students regularly underestimate themselves) and, if not, what changes need to be made.

You may wish to ask the students to complete the quiz again after a period of a few months, to see if their scores have changed and to reflect on the areas where they have made improvements.

How can speaking and listening skills be improved?

Activity 6 Reading the letters independently will give students the opportunity to practise their skills of identifying key points in a text, although discussion of the problems with a partner or a small group should be encouraged afterwards. In discussing the problems and in finding solutions, students should develop an awareness of how to improve their own Speaking and listening skills.

Writing the replies will provide practice in matching tone to audience and purpose and could be set as a homework task. Students should look back at the criteria in the quiz questions to give them guidance in writing replies. They should also be encouraged to offer more informal and practical advice.

Here are some suggestions students could make in their replies:

Text D:

- Use cards for your notes, not A4 paper, as this might encourage you to write too much and then read it.
- Make sure your notes are very short so there is not much to read: no more than three points on one card.

Text E:

- Write a plan for your presentation to make sure you include enough points.
- Read your presentation aloud as you are writing it. This will increase your confidence if you do it often enough.
- Practise your presentation with a friend or a relative who can help you by telling you when to vary your tone of voice and when to look up at the audience.

Text F:

- Make sure you let your group know how you feel so they can choose a role you are comfortable with.
- Begin by taking on a small part in a role play to build up your confidence.
- Remember that creating a character does not just mean using your voice – it also means using body language and gesture.

- Practise your role play with a relative or friend who will give you advice about how to alter your tone of voice and create movements and gestures suitable for your character.

Review and reflect

Students should be encouraged to look back at their scores in Activity 5 to help them set their targets. Some may need guidance in setting realistic targets. For example, if a student has difficulty in creating a memorable character in role plays (5–7), there is little point in them selecting a role-play comment from the highest level of achievement (14–15). They should select their target from the range above, for example, 'use language and gesture to create characters'.

Their responses in this section should be recorded in their Speaking and listening portfolio, so that they can refer to and review their targets on a regular basis.

Outcomes

Learning activity: Speaking and listening terminology

In this chapter your students have:

- thought carefully about the skills needed by good speakers and listeners
- practised their listening skills
- identified their strengths as a speaker and listener
- reflected on ways to improve their speaking and listening
- given advice to others on how to improve.

25 Presenting

AO focus

English AO1 Speaking and listening and English Language AO1 Speaking and listening.

- Speak to communicate clearly and purposefully; structure and sustain talk, adapting it to different situations and audiences; use Standard English and a variety of techniques as appropriate.
- Listen and respond to speakers' ideas, perspectives and how they construct and express their meanings.
- Interact with others, shaping meanings through suggestions, comments and questions and drawing ideas together.
- Create and sustain different roles.

In this chapter your students will:

- explore features of effective presentations
- explore appropriate kinds of language to use in presentations
- consider how to structure presentations.

Additional resources

Worksheets

25a: Presentations: openings
25b: PowerPoint
25c: Speeches

Getting started

Students are probably familiar with the idea of making presentations, but often their preparatory focus is on the content of their presentation rather than its structure or the style of their delivery. The focus in this chapter will be on techniques and the development of skills that will help students present content more effectively.

It is worthwhile noting that the highest band of achievement in the assessment criteria for 'creating and sustaining roles' refers to 'performances and presentations'. This suggests that presenting is a role, just as being a chairperson is a role. That is why the starting point is to look at that role.

Activity 1 focuses students on the role of the presenter and should be used as a starting point.

Working through the chapter

Making presentations

Students will eventually be assessed on the basis of one presentation they make, but it would be good practice to ensure that they deliver a variety of presentations – on their own, as a pair, as part of a small group – to a variety of audiences, real and imagined, for a variety of purposes.

Activity 1 Students may focus on things like assemblies, but they will probably be used to making and listening to presentations in quite a wide range of subjects.

Ideas could be exchanged in small groups and collated on the board. You will expect a focus on:

- body language
- eye contact
- modulation of voice
- concise, interesting content
- clear structure
- use of humour when appropriate.

Following this activity, small groups could make posters: 'Top 10 tips for effective presentations to a teenage audience'. They could then be invited to discuss how they might, as a group, make a presentation to their peers about making presentations. The challenge would be to avoid simply reading a list: they could be invited to suggest strategies for making the presentation engaging and effective.

Standard English

Learning activity: A changing language

It would be worthwhile referring to Chapter 25 of the Student Book, in which students explore Standard English, dialect and accent. Ability to use Standard English is specified in assessment criteria in all five bands of the 'communicating and adapting language' column, but from Band 2 upwards it is always qualified by words like 'appropriate' or 'where necessary'. Despite the difficulties of defining Standard English, most students will know the difference between what is generally considered 'correct' and dialects.

Standard English is quite a complex area – there are different standard forms, for example – so it would be a mistake to spend a lot of time exploring its nature, but two simple messages could be emphasised:

- it does not concern accent
- at a simple level, Standard English is what is generally perceived to be grammatically and lexically correct. If there is an understanding of what slang and colloquial mean, there will be an appreciation of the norm that slang and colloquial uses of language differ from.

Activity 2 This should be fairly straightforward. The Standard English version is:

- 'He was going to the pub.'

There could be discussion of 'pub'. Some may consider it to be non-standard because it is a shortened form of public house, but it is so commonly used that it must be considered standard.

Standard usage would be:

a 'I **was** wearing **the** red **hat** and he **was** wearing **the** green **one**.'
b 'We should put **our** names **in the** book.'
c '**Our brother**.'
d 'Are **you** going out?'

Activity 3 This could be a whole-class activity, with examples being written down on the board. It would be worthwhile briefly discussing why – in what circumstances – there might be a need to avoid such usage.

Activity 4 The examples are not intended to be difficult; they are simply ways of getting students to engage with the idea of what 'appropriate' means: discussion should focus on audience and purpose. Students could be asked to generalise from these examples – under what circumstances is it appropriate to use:

- Standard English?
- non-standard versions of the language?

Using a range of language

Many students will, without guidance, use the same register and tone whatever the audience and purpose. They should be made to think about explicitly selecting vocabulary and expression to meet a variety of situations. It would be a good idea to link this to their writing: just as they select vocabulary and vary sentence structures to engage a reader, they should be encouraged to think carefully about vocabulary choices in their speaking.

It would be best if a student read the two made-up presentations.

Students might not like the second presentation; they might find it to be too self-consciously crafted, a bit of an embarrassment. The purpose of the two examples, however, is to draw attention to the fact that the second speaker is, at least, trying to bring some variety to the talk – there is some sense of style – whereas the first is thoughtlessly dull.

Structuring your presentation
Beginning

k! Video case study activity: Presentations

k! Analysis activity: Studying speeches

Activity 5 This should not take very long, but it would be a good idea to stress the importance of a good beginning to a presentation and to share ways of avoiding stating the obvious. How to greet an audience – real or imagined – is worth consideration. Students could discuss how to establish a tone: Will the presentation be light-hearted or serious? Which opening would best establish the chosen tone? Worksheet 25a can be used to further reinforce what makes a good opening to a presentation.

Key points

Activity 6 It will be difficult to hear more than a handful of examples. The key features to focus on are:

- how well the key point is headlined
- how it is then developed.

As students feed back, the class should be listening carefully to how different speakers introduce their key point, develop it and then move on to the second point. Students may have worked on Chapter 7 in the Reading section of the book. In that chapter they explored the idea of 'key points' in writing. If students understand that a 'key point' in a paragraph of writing is the main idea that can be concisely described, and that sentences in a paragraph develop and explore that one main idea, it will help them to make the link between their speaking and writing.

If there is access to a camera, students could make 15-second presentations to camera, expressing their opinion about a film. Run together it could make an entertaining and instructive video. It would be best if several students spoke about the same film.

Ending

Endings are not as important as beginnings, but it would be worthwhile discussing the difference between stopping – just running out of material – and concluding – bringing the presentation to an effective end, perhaps by summarising, reminding, before inviting questions where appropriate.

Using PowerPoint

Poor use of Microsoft PowerPoint or other presentational software has killed many a presentation and students are subjected to its use on many occasions. They should be able to compile their own lists of 'Do' and 'Don't' points when using it (Worksheet 25b).

Body language and voice

Appropriate and inappropriate body language could emerge from the discussion of presentational software – for example, not turning your back on your audience. Students should discuss eye contact – what they think is effective and what does not work. Adolescents may point out their difficulties in establishing eye contact with certain members of their student audience, but they should also be able to generalise about the significance of establishing eye contact – some professional advice will suggest establishing quick eye contact with virtually everyone in an audience.

Activity 7 Students could be expected to suggest that it would best to:

- **avoid:** looking down, turning your back, fidgeting nervously, moving around too much, anything that might distract, such as constantly playing with hair, slouching
- **adopt:** eye contact, standing largely still, looking ahead, smiling.

Activity 8

Learning activity: A news presentation

This activity is intended to bring things together. It is important that students work through the different stages rather than simply taking the title 'Five things I hate about …' and immediately preparing their talk. The title is arbitrary – it could just as easily be 'Five things I love about …'.

As this is to be delivered to the class, it would be a good idea to set up some peer assessment. This could be achieved by simply inviting responses, but it might be better to appoint someone as a 'buddy' to the student presenter and ask the buddy to give feedback when appropriate.

Feedback should be carefully focused on:

- how well the talk engaged the listener
- how well structured it was
- any particularly effective uses of language
- how body language and voice were used.

Stretch yourself

The activity at the end is simply a suggestion for an activity that could be an assessable piece of work. It would be up to students to plan for it, using some of the skills they have explored through the chapter. Alternatively, you could use Worksheet 25c, which asks students to analyse a speech by Martin Luther King.

Outcomes

In this chapter your students have:

- thought about appropriate kinds of language to use in presentations
- explored ways of organising and delivering presentations
- delivered a presentation.

26 Discussing and listening

AO focus

English AO1 Speaking and listening and English Language AO3 Speaking and listening.

- Interact with others.
- Speak to communicate clearly and purposefully.
- Listen and respond to speakers' ideas and perspectives.

In this chapter your students will:

- practise the skills needed to be a supportive listener
- develop the skills needed for partner work
- learn how to contribute to work in a small group.

Getting started

As an activity to raise students' awareness of group interaction, you could ask students to draw up a list of all the groups in which they function, for example:

- family groups
- groups of friends
- sports teams.

This could be followed up by asking students to note three things about the ways in which their different groups share ideas. Both positive and negative comments could be included.

An additional starter could be to ask students to identify what they like about working in groups and what they find difficult. Some of the difficulties identified could be:

- Everyone talks at once, I can't work out what's going on.
- I find it difficult to get my point across.
- I find it difficult to think of things to say.

Once the difficulties have been aired you could discuss with students different ways of getting round them. After the guidelines for working in groups have been drawn up the difficulties should have been addressed.

Working through the chapter

At the outset it must be stressed to students that working in groups is a very important skill and one in which they are expected to make progress throughout Key Stage 4.

For some students, productive work in groups can be difficult. Some find it hard to keep on task, whereas some are happy to leave it to others to make contributions. On the other hand, it can be very rewarding for students to take part in a successful group activity or performance.

One key to the success of group work is the make-up of the group. You should think carefully about the organisation of groups for the activities in this chapter. Students who are close friends do not always work well together, even in partner activities. Sometimes a very articulate student is able to give confidence to a more reserved student. On occasions it is helpful to more able students to allow them to work in a group with students of similar ability. On other occasions mixed-ability groups work well, particularly in developing those who are less able, as they receive stimulus and ideas from those who are more able.

Working together

Before starting the activities you may find it useful to ask students to draw up their own guidelines for working in groups. Here are some suggestions they could make:

- Take turns in talking.
- Do not interrupt anyone if they are talking.
- Do not use put-downs if you don't agree with someone's point.
- Challenge someone politely if you don't agree with them.
- Appoint a chairperson to organise the discussion and to make sure everyone has their turn.
- Ask someone in the group to make a note of points as you go along.
- Keep to agreed time limits.
- Make sure everyone has their say, including quiet people.

After students have worked in groups you may wish to hold a whole-class plenary, so that guidelines can be shared and a set of guidelines from the whole class can be agreed.

Activity 1 There is no set order for the listening skills. The purpose of the activity is to get students to focus on the skills required to be an active listener. You could also ask them to give reasons for the order they have chosen. They could consider whether the order of the skills might change according to the group they

English and English Language Teacher's Book Higher Tier
Section C: Speaking and listening

are working in. For example, in a one-to-one interview, listening sensitively might be at the top of the list.

Activity 2 Although students are instructed not to plan their talks, they may find it useful to think briefly about three things that get on their nerves so that they don't run out of things to say. It does not matter if they do not refer to all three in their short talk.

Following the activity you could ask students to reflect on how easy or difficult it was for them to listen to their partner. Some students may say they found it hard to concentrate, others that they can't remember easily the two or three things they were asked to report to another group. They could also identify ways to overcome their difficulties. One way to do this would be to make an effort to remember something from the first few seconds of the talk. Those who wait until the end may find it harder to remember what was said at the beginning.

When students have to report back to another pair on what they have heard, this will extend their listening skills still further.

Developing questioning skills

k! Learning activity: Question types

It should be made clear to the students from the outset that there is a link between listening skills and questioning skills. Students who ask appropriately detailed questions are those who have listened carefully to a presentation or to other speakers in a group situation. It should also be made clear to them that by asking appropriate questions they are helping their classmates to expand on their ideas and to improve the quality of their talk.

Activity 3 Before tackling this activity, you may wish to ensure that students are very clear about the difference between open and closed questions, perhaps by asking them a series of short questions and asking them to state whether they are open or closed. For example:

- Do you enjoy school? – closed.
- What do you enjoy most about coming to school? – open.

Responses to the examples given in the Student Book are as follows:

- 'That must be so annoying, but maybe it's entertaining as well? Can you tell us about any funny things he has done?' – open.
- 'Has he stopped doing this now?' – closed.
- 'Could you give me any more examples of naughty things he has done?' – open, as it invites students to carry on talking.

- 'When you are older what will you remember most about your little brother and why?' – open.

Activity 4 Before students continue the activity by asking questions of other speakers, you may want to give them time to plan their questions. This will reinforce the importance of questioning/listening skills, as well as ensuring that questions are open ones and will encourage further talk.

Students should be encouraged to provide feedback to their partners on how helpful they found the questions. Following this they could set their own targets for improvement.

Working with a partner

k! Video case study activity: An interview

Before showing students the list of skills and qualities needed when working with a partner, you may wish to ask them to identify their own, which could then be checked against the list in the Student Book.

Activity 5 You may wish to stress to students at the beginning of this activity that they are working with a partner to reach a shared decision and that in some cases a compromise will be needed.

They should be reminded to follow the guidelines very precisely, to avoid drifting away from the focus of the task. Setting a clear time limit for the task (10–15 minutes) would also improve focus. If they wish, students could make brief notes as they follow the bullet points. A further stage in the activity could be an explanation of the reasons for the chosen charity, given to the whole class.

You could also conduct a class vote to determine which charity was determined as the most popular.

Review and reflect

The aim of the activity is not to encourage competition among students, but to enable them to reflect honestly on their achievements in the partner task and to work out their strengths and weaknesses. The maximum score is 15 and the minimum score is 5. Once students have scored themselves, they could show their response to the partner they worked with to see whether their scores are an honest reflection of their performance.

Following this, students could be asked to make brief notes on the partner task in their Speaking and listening portfolio, together with their scores and targets for improvement, which should be based on the five statements used for scoring their performance.

Chapter 26
Discussing and listening

Working in a group

(k!) Learning activity: Group roles

(k!) Analysis activity: Transcript analysis

A suggested number for a group is four or five students, with the observer as an additional student – perhaps one borrowed from another group. Groups larger than five can become unmanageable and may result in some students being overlooked.

In addition to electing a chairperson to guide a group through activities and keep them on task, it can also be useful to appoint an observer. The role of the observer should be to note positive features of interaction, such as one student drawing another into the discussion, praising the contribution of another or making a point that takes the discussion in another direction. The role of the observer can also be helpful to students when they are setting targets for improvement.

The reporter for the group (see part (b) of Activity 6) should be elected at the outset. This can be an unpopular role, as students sometimes think being a reporter means they cannot express their opinion, which should not be the case. It should be stressed that the whole group has a responsibility to contribute to the reporter's account.

Activity 6

a   Once again it should be made clear that the results of the discussion should be the consensus of the whole group. This is a collaborative task and reaching a group-agreed decision will almost certainly require some compromise.

It is important to stress that the discussion should be thorough. Both advantages and disadvantages of each suggestion should be explored.

b   As with the group decision, the preparation of the group report is a shared task. The reporter is not a student who has to do extra work, but one who has taken on the role of acting as spokesperson for the whole group.

Once the report has been given to the whole class, you may wish to extend the session by inviting questions that could be answered by any member of the group.

Review and reflect

The student self-assessment carried out here could be recorded in a Speaking and listening portfolio. It is important that students focus appropriately on things that did not go well in order to identify ways to improve to achieve progression in Speaking and listening.

Outcomes

In this chapter your students have:

- developed their questioning skills
- practised listening with concentration
- expressed and developed their own opinions in partner and group tasks
- responded to the ideas of a partner, challenging them where necessary
- worked collaboratively with others in a group to discuss ideas and reach a conclusion.

27 Creating and sustaining roles

AO focus

English AO1 Speaking and listening and English Language AO1 Speaking and listening.

- Create and sustain different roles.

In this chapter your students will:

- learn what is meant by 'roles'
- learn how voice, vocabulary and gesture help shape a role
- create roles and receive feedback on their effectiveness.

Getting started

Role playing is one of three compulsory elements of Unit 2 assessment. In the previous specification this was called 'drama-focused activity', and the new title clarifies that the focus is on assuming a role. Guidance suggests that the idea of 'role' will now include activities such as being the chair of a discussion group, but the focus in this chapter is on dramatic role.

Students are probably invited to take on a role quite often – in a hot-seating activity, for example – but it may be the case that they spend only a small amount of time considering dramatic techniques. This chapter is intended to introduce students to some of the techniques they might consider when assuming an identity other than their own.

The assessment criteria in Band 4 refer to 'a range of carefully selected verbal and non-verbal techniques', and it is worthwhile stressing the significance of 'non-verbal' to students. This is, after all, an assessment in speaking and listening, but creating and sustaining a role brings a wider range of skills into play than use of voice.

It would be a good idea to begin with a focus on 'character'. Students could be invited to share opinions on characters in films, books, plays or television programmes. The basic question would be:

- What makes an invented character interesting/engaging?

This could be undertaken in small groups or as a whole class. Students could be asked to select a character from a soap opera and then discuss which aspects of the characterisation are interesting.

To introduce some element of evaluation, they could also be invited to draw attention to characters who are considered uninteresting.

When some 'interesting' characters have been selected, the discussion should focus on what an actor (or writer) does to make that characterisation come to life.

Another activity that would be a useful starting point would be to look carefully at very small snippets of television or film drama to put acting methodology under the microscope. The focus should be on voice, gesture and vocabulary.

Working through the chapter

Creating a role

It is worthwhile spending some time discussing with students what 'role' means in Speaking and listening. Professionally scripted roles are not allowed: students cannot be assessed if they learn some dialogue from, say, a Shakespeare play. They may, however, take an existing role from a published play and develop that character using their own words.

It is important to draw students' attention to the assessment criteria:

Band	Creating and sustaining roles
1	• draw on obvious and sometimes stereotypical ideas to create simple characters • react to situations in predictable but appropriate ways, demonstrating some understanding of relationships and familiar ideas
2	• show understanding of characters by creating straightforward roles using speech, gesture and movement • engage with situations and ideas, showing understanding of issues and relationships
3	• develop and sustain roles and characters through appropriate language and effective gesture and movement • make contributions to the development of situations and ideas, showing understanding and insight into relationships and significant issues
4	• create convincing characters and roles using a range of carefully selected verbal and non-verbal techniques • respond skillfully and sensitively in different situations and scenarios, to explore ideas, issues and relationships
5	• create complex characters and fulfil the demands of challenging roles through insightful choice of dramatic approaches • explore and respond to complex ideas, issues and relationships in varied formal and informal scenarios.

The key terminology is the move from 'simple' to 'complex', and it would be good to discuss this with students: what makes for simple and complex characterisation? It would be useful if students decided for themselves that complex might suggest a multifaceted character. It could be a good idea to introduce the idea of 'stereotype' as being 'simple' rather than complex.

Character

Analysis activity: Finding characters

Case study activity: Characters of the imagination

In creating and sustaining a role, students will assume the identity of a character. The activities in this section of the chapter focus on techniques that can be used to create a character.

Voice

Activity 1 It will be important to explore just what different students do with their voice and body language. If students are to learn the skills of developing a role, they need to be given some tools of the trade, so it will not be enough for a student to enact a 'challenging' way of expressing a word; those watching need to be able to describe what they have seen and heard – something that they could replicate.

It would be a good idea to develop a classroom display based on digital photographs of students enacting words in particular ways. The photographs could be annotated.

Activities 2 and 3 The main classroom challenge here is how to manage 20-plus students all doing this! There will need to be some selection of those who are going to perform. Perhaps it would be a good idea to produce these small dramas in groups of three, with only one student actually performing. The point is that this is practice for watchers to learn techniques from.

It would be a good idea to keep these two activities separate from Activity 4 so there can be explicit focus on voice and then body.

Gesture

Activity 4 It would be a good idea before students embark on this activity to construct a list of different emotions. As each is put on the board, a student could be invited to give a quick response as to how the emotion could be shown through body language. Feedback should draw attention to precise details of what students did to convey the range of emotions.

Activity 5

a Students can work in groups to analyse the images. Encourage them to back up their ideas with reasons.

b Other suggestions might include opening arms or holding out hands as a sign of welcome or openness.

c This could be digitally photographed, with separate photographs being annotated to draw attention to the body language and facial gestures which reveal a particular trait. The photographs could be printed and displayed.

d Some examples include:
- Students could model appropriate and inappropriate ways of sitting for an interview, from the slouched attitude that suggests lack of interest, to an over-formal, straight-backed pose that suggests a rabbit caught in the headlights.
- Students could model poses that suggest authority in teachers.
- The 'chat-up' body language could be presented as tableaux by pairs of students.

All three examples should be treated fairly light-heartedly.

Vocabulary

Activity 6

a Sorry: 'soz', 'pardon', 'my fault', 'oops', 'forgive', plus variations of how to say sorry by stressing different parts of the word in different ways.

I don't understand: 'what?', 'you what?', 'eh?', 'sorry?', 'don't get you'.

That's great: 'brill', 'ace', 'cool', 'wonderful', 'fab', 'smashing'.

There should be discussion about what kind of character in what kind of situation might use the different versions of the words.

b The focus here is on simply capturing the kinds of language used by different kinds of people. The purpose of the translator is to bring a touch of humour and to draw attention to the differences between standard and non-standard uses of English that can help characterisation.

Activity 7

a It is important that students understand why this little piece of drama is to be enacted while sitting down. The focus is on voice, vocabulary and limited body language – facial gestures will be important. There should be a reminder

English and English Language Teacher's Book Higher Tier
Section C: Speaking and listening

about the target of a 'complex character': complexity may be helped by some careful and imaginative planning of the course of the interview. Pairs need to create the opportunity for variety of response.

b Perhaps the most important part of this activity is the discussion of performance: it should be possible to tease out specific gestures, words and tone of voice used for characterisation. Comment should be based on precise details and couched in supportive language.

Working in a small group

Most students will work in groups when they are creating and sustaining a role, and it is important that they understand how important the group dynamic is in producing short pieces of effective drama: complex characterisation may depend on the interplay between characters. If anger is to be a feature of one role, there needs to be consideration of how that anger is to be provoked. One character may only be able to demonstrate a certain aspect of their character by feeding off lines delivered by another.

There are issues of differentiation to be considered: teachers will need to decide which mix of students may lead to the best results. A very powerful piece of characterisation by one gifted student could put others in a group in the shade. A group of two may suit some students better than a group of five.

Activity 8 The small-group discussion of how to develop this group role play could be an opportunity for the assessment of a Discussing and listening task. Key issues for the groups are to:

- ensure that each group member has an equal chance of creating a role
- develop a 'story' that they can dramatise
- explore interactions between characters that will allow each character to develop interestingly.

Again, it will be very important for the class, as audience, to feed back their response to the various characterisations.

Using literary texts

Audio role-play activity: In the hotseat

Using literary texts that have been read/studied by the students is an obvious route to pursue, both for effective Unit 2 tasks and for study of the text.

Activity 9 There is a practical issue to manage: is there time to watch 20-plus examples of hot-seating? It may be best to use hot-seating at various stages of the course, with students working in small groups and only a small number being assessed at any one time.

Hot-seating is, of course, a very useful tool for exploring a text, but if a student produces a wonderful but textually inaccurate performance, that should not in any way count against them for assessment of Unit 2. Characters in a novel like *Of Mice and Men* arguably lack much 'complexity', so a bit of creativity might be a very good idea for the purposes of Speaking and listening.

It will help to share good ideas for questions with the class: questions that allow the student in character to respond effectively.

Monologues can work especially well when performed to camera without much of an audience. Use of simple headshots will give a focus on tone of voice and facial gestures. It could be especially effective to use the camera as the listener – the camera as a character who is being spoken to. Such opportunities may serve the more introverted student well.

Activity 10 The suggestions may be helpful ways of exploring a variety of texts, but the main focus should be on student performance rather than insight into the text. A modern version of Capulet's verbal assault on Juliet in *Romeo and Juliet* would be judged on the interest of the roles rather than on their proximity to Shakespeare's characters. It is, of course, inappropriate to assess students using the exact words of a literary text for Unit 2.

This activity would be best approached as a small-group activity. If, for example, the class had been studying a text like *Romeo and Juliet*, different small groups could be asked to devise 'missing' scenes which focus on different characters – one on Romeo, one on Juliet, one on Tybalt, and so on. That would make the presentation of the different scenes more practical than every group approaching the same scene or the same character.

Outcomes

In this chapter your students have:

- considered what a 'role' is
- explored how voice, vocabulary and body language can help shape a role
- created different roles in different situations.

28 Making your speaking and listening skills count in the controlled assessment

AO focus

English AO1 Speaking and listening and English Language AO3 Speaking and listening.

- Speak to communicate clearly and purposefully; structure and sustain talk, adapting it to different situations and audiences; use Standard English and a variety of techniques as appropriate.
- Listen and respond to speakers' ideas and perspectives and how they construct and express meanings.
- Interact with others, shaping meanings through suggestions, comments and questions and drawing ideas together.
- Create and sustain different roles.

In this chapter your students will:

- learn about how speaking and listening fits into their GCSE course
- explore the Assessment Objective for speaking and listening
- look at the types of task they might undertake.

Additional resources

Worksheets

28a: Key words

Working through the chapter

What is controlled assessment?

The controlled assessment is new to GCSE teachers in all subjects. However, the Speaking and listening element of GCSE English and GCSE English Language, although referred to as controlled assessment, does retain many elements familiar to those who have already taught GCSE. The first paragraph of the Student Book chapter explains to students how the formal Speaking and listening assessment fits into their GCSE course.

The overall aims and outcomes of the course include enabling learners to:

- demonstrate skills in speaking and listening necessary to communicate with others confidently, effectively, precisely and appropriately
- express themselves creatively and imaginatively
- understand the patterns, structures and conventions of spoken English
- select and adapt speech to different situations and audiences.

It might be useful to contextualise the idea of the Speaking and listening controlled assessment for your students, making clear to them the value of this aspect of the course, not only to their GCSE grade but to their overall ability to communicate in the wider world. Your centre will already have a range of Speaking and listening assessments; you will be aware that this aspect of the course is very similar in terms of type of assessment to those undertaken in the past.

You will perhaps want to outline that although there is a requirement for three formal assessments, there will be other opportunities for developing Speaking and listening skills during the course of their lessons. Also, it may be useful to highlight the fact that Speaking and listening assessments are not 'exams' – although they demand rigour, their very nature will be different from a written controlled assessment, and students will need to understand that these assessments require the same level of application as other assessed aspects of their GCSE. Stressing that 20 per cent of their overall grade will be awarded for Speaking and listening will help students to perceive the importance of achieving highly in this unit of the course.

Students may well have questions at this point, especially if your centre has not undertaken formal assessments of Speaking and listening at Key Stage 3.

Introducing the tasks

Activity 4 of the Student Book is a recall activity. If resources are available, it may be useful to display the following vocabulary at this point in the lesson:

> presenting   sophisticated   assured   interview
> three   skilful   sensitive and thoughtful
> characters   roles   convincing   analysing
> developing   adapting   exploring   shaping
> flexible   appropriate   discussing   listening
> speaking

109

This section of the Student Book explains the three headings under which the Speaking and listening tasks will fall:

- Presenting
- Discussing and listening
- Role playing.

Next there are definitions provided of what a good speaker and a good listener should be. However, before looking at these definitions in the Student Book, this could be an appropriate moment to ask students the question: What do we mean by speaking and listening? You could encourage them to spend a few minutes devising their own definitions of the two terms, along with some examples of how they may be assessed or the types of qualities that may be rewarded at assessment.

The section that follows breaks down the Assessment Objectives, analysing each element in turn and providing further clarification for students.

The Assessment Objectives are the same for both GCSE English and GCSE English Language. They can appear daunting, as they are written for teachers and other professionals; therefore it might be useful to break them down into smaller sections for students – or ask the students to break them down themselves into more numerous, smaller AOs.

Another useful task might be to take some descriptors from the mark scheme for Speaking and listening and ask pairs of students to rank the skills vocabulary into grade bands. There are five grade bands in the specification mark scheme, each with a word or phrase designed to give general exemplification of qualities for that band:

- **Band 1:** 1–3 marks (limited)
- **Band 2:** 4–6 marks (some)
- **Band 3:** 7–9 marks (clear, consistent)
- **Band 4:** 10–12 marks (confident, assured)
- **Band 5:** 13–15 marks (sophisticated, impressive).

For example, strand one of the 'communicating and adapting language' (Presenting) task progresses through the mark bands as follows:

- **Band 1:** briefly express points of view, ideas and feelings
- **Band 2:** convey straightforward information and ideas, coherent accounts and narratives in extended turns
- **Band 3:** effectively communicate information, ideas and feelings, promote issues and points of view

- **Band 4:** confidently convey and interpret information, ideas and feelings, emphasising significant points and issues
- **Band 5:** highlight priorities and essential detail when communicating complex and demanding subject-matter.

Another task might be to ask students to rephrase the AOs into more student-friendly language. This has already been done with the highlighted sections of the AO criteria, but you may want to take that further with your students. Perhaps they could take this section of the chapter and devise a presentation to a younger audience – possibly a Year 7 or 8 group – on how to achieve a good grade for Speaking and listening. However you decide to approach this, it is very important that the students have a clear idea of what the AOs actually mean.

Your centre will already have the record-keeping paperwork in place for Speaking and listening, as it was a requirement of the old specification. It might be that your centre has already revised and adapted this paperwork in the light of a fresh specification. You will need to give the students some idea of the type of task and the type of groupings that are allowed for each. You may want to explain that the examination board provides 'limited control' guidance on the nature of tasks to be undertaken for Speaking and listening, but it is the centre which sets the tasks. AQA provide record-keeping documents to allow the teacher to record brief notes and details of activities undertaken.

Sample tasks and sample answers

Students will need to complete a minimum of three formal Speaking and listening controlled assessments under the headings mentioned above.

The controlled assessment criteria refer to skills areas for each heading, which clarifies things even further:

- **Presenting:** Communicating and adapting language
- **Discussing and listening:** Interacting and responding
- **Role playing:** Creating and sustaining roles.

Presenting

Planning activity: The Speaking and listening controlled assessment 1

This section of the Student Book gives more detail about the marking criteria for the Presenting task, along with some exemplar tasks. The skills criteria are all taken from Band 4, which is notional B/A.

Some key words have been emboldened for students to focus in particular on the skills. Also, corresponding key words from Band 5 have been included in order that students compare the different layers of skills necessary for moving through the mark bands.

Activity 1 This activity asks students to look at two texts – A and B – which are both descriptions of students undertaking a Presenting task (in this case, a formal presentation to the class for the Room 101 activity). Students are asked first to decide which of the two texts would achieve the most marks. In this case, Text A would achieve a higher mark than Text B.

The second part of this activity involves students providing some advice for Student A in order for them to achieve a higher grade. Students could work in pairs for this activity, looking at the criteria for Presenting which was broken down for them in the earlier part of the chapter.

Discussing and listening

Connecting comments activity: The Speaking and listening controlled assessment 2

This section of the Student Book gives more detail about the marking criteria for the Discussing and listening task, along with some exemplar tasks. The skills criteria are all taken from Band 4, which is notional B/A. Some key words have also been highlighted for students to focus in particular on the skills. Also, corresponding key words from Band 5 have been included in order that students compare the different layers of skills necessary for moving through the mark bands.

Activity 2 This activity asks students to look at two texts – Texts C and D – (in this case, which are both descriptions of students undertaking a Discussing and listening task, a student working in a group situation on the Sports Day task). They are asked to decide which student would receive the higher mark – in this case the student in Text C.

Role playing

On your marks activity: The Speaking and listening controlled assessment 3

This section of the Student Book gives more detail about the marking criteria for the Role-playing task, along with some exemplar tasks. The skills criteria are all taken from Band 4, which is notional B/A. Some key words have been highlighted for students to focus in particular on the skills. Also, corresponding key words from Band 5 have been included in order that students compare the different layers of skills necessary for moving through the mark bands.

Activity 3 This activity asks students to look at two texts – E and F – which are both descriptions of students undertaking a role-playing task. Again their task is to decide which student would achieve a higher mark – in this case, Text E.

Once students have completed Activities 1–3, you might want to ask them to consider the three exemplar tasks for each heading (Presenting, Discussing and listening, and Role playing), and then to work either in pairs or in a small group to devise their own further task for one of the headings.

Activity 4 (Worksheet 28a) This activity provides a selection of the key Assessment Objective vocabulary for students to study for a short period before seeing how many they can remember. If you have a projector or whiteboard available and have started off the lesson with the vocabulary from this activity, you could leave it prominently displayed during the lesson, before giving your students one last chance to look at it before switching off/covering up and asking them to jot down as many words as they can remember, then share with a partner, then check back with the display to see what they have missed.

Of course, there are many other ways in which you might want to encourage your students to sum up what they have learned from this chapter. For example, you might want them each to take a minute to write a question about this aspect of the course on small pieces of paper, which are all placed in a 'hat' for redistribution and answered by another student.

Outcomes

In this chapter your students have:

- learned about the importance of speaking and listening as a part of their GCSE course
- learned more about the ways they can achieve high marks in this part of the course.

Section D: Spoken language

Overview

Section D of the Student Book is designed to develop students' skills in spoken language as defined by the Assessment Objectives for GCSE English Language (AO2 Study of spoken language) and tested in the controlled assessments.

GCSE English Language: AO2 Study of spoken language

- Understand variations in spoken language, explaining why language changes in relation to contexts.
- Evaluate the impact of spoken language choices in their own and others' use.

The chapters provide opportunities for students to develop their skills in an area generally not studied at an earlier stage in an English course. The learning objectives, founded in the Assessment Objectives but in 'student-friendly' language, are given at the start of each chapter. Throughout each chapter the learning points are clarified and modelled, and followed by activities that are designed to reinforce and extend students' learning.

Students are encouraged to work independently or in pairs or small groups, as appropriate, and are given regular opportunities to assess their personal progress and that of other students, often against fixed criteria. While many of the activities are exploratory, the learning within the chapters is designed to be cumulative, building on what has come before. In both chapters, the extension activities at the end lead students into a new area for exploration.

Each chapter can be used as a discrete stand-alone topic, with activities and tasks specific to the named objectives. The order in which they appear in the Student Book does not have to be followed, though it is worth noting that this order was arrived at after careful consideration of how best to build students' skills in the study of spoken language.

Assessment

> *GCSE English Language*
>
> **Controlled assessment title:** Studying spoken language
>
> **Mark value:** 10% = 20 marks
>
> **Choice of task:** One of:
> - Social attitudes to spoken language
> - Spoken genres
> - Multi-modal talk.
>
> **Planning and preparation:** Students are allowed to spend time discussing the texts and task, and they may make brief notes which can be taken into the controlled assessment.
>
> **Time for writing:** 2–3 hours
>
> **Expected length:** 800–1000 words

Section D
Spoken language

Nelson Thornes resources

Chapter	Student Book activities	kerboodle! resources
29: Choosing and using language	1–2: Paired and group work using speech in different situations and noting differences between the speech used 3: Making notes on how purpose and audience affect spoken language 4: Preparing a transcript of a conversation/speech 5: Identifying features of idiolect 6–7: Identifying features of sociolect 8: Suggesting other influences on idiolect 9–10: Analysing the language used in speeches Stretch yourself: Investigating the idiolect of an elderly person; analysing the delivery of Obama's inaugural speech	• Audio case study activity: Transcripts • Analysis activity: Dialect • Webquest activity: Exploring dialect • Learning activity: Jargon • Learning activity: Speeches • Worksheet 29a: Purpose and audience
30: Multi-modal talk	1: Making notes on language use and identifying which involved spoken language and/or written language 2: Sorting features of spoken and written language 3: Placing forms of language use on a continuum to show which are spoken forms and which are written forms 4: Group discussion to work out the conventions of texting 5: Writing a guide to texting in the early 21st century 6: Identifying concerns about texting and prioritising these 7–8: Analysing an instant messaging 'conversation' Stretch yourself: Writing an article about the dangers of chatroom use and how these could be mitigated	• Learning activity: Language modes • Analysis activity: Urban bee-keeping • Learning activity: Features of spoken language • Analysis activity: Creative texting • Viewpoints activity: Texting – good or bad? • Worksheet 30a: Differences between written and spoken language • Worksheet 30b: Full MSN chat
31: Making your spoken language study skills count in the controlled assessment	1: Identifying how part of a sample response to a 'Social attitudes to spoken language' task can be improved 2: Analysing the language used in part of a sample response to a 'Spoken genres' task 3: Writing a paragraph based on part of a sample response to a 'Multi-modal talk' task to explain the terminology of texting and its effects	• On your marks activity: The Spoken language study controlled assessment 1 • On your marks activity: The Spoken language study controlled assessment 2 • Planning activity: The Spoken language study controlled assessment 3 • Worksheet 31a: Spoken genres

English and English Language Teacher's Book Higher Tier
Section D: Spoken language

Student checklist worksheet

Use the questions below to assess your spoken language skills and to set your personal spoken language targets.

Skill	Very confident	Quite confident	Sometimes I can	Often I can't	Which chapters might help?
Analyse different types of speech					29
Explain how speech is influenced by purpose and audience					29
Explain why language changes depending on the context in which it is being used					29, 30
Identify different genres of spoken language					30

Use your responses to the checklist to set yourself *no more than* three targets to achieve from the Spoken language section.

1. ....

2. ....

3. ....

Section D
Spoken language

Checking students' progress

The tasks below are all included in the Student Book and can be used to check student progress in a particular skill.

Chapters	AO focus	Activities from Student Book and learning outcomes
29	<ul><li>Understand variations in spoken language, explaining why language changes in relation to contexts</li><li>Evaluate the impact of spoken language choices in their own and others' use</li></ul>	**Chapter 29, Activity 9** Students:<ul><li>analyse language from a speech</li><li>refer to the features used and the effect that they have.</li></ul>
30	<ul><li>Understand variations in spoken language, explaining why language changes in relation to contexts</li><li>Evaluate the impact of spoken language choices in their own and others' use</li></ul>	**Chapter 30, Activity 8** Students:<ul><li>identify features of language used in instant messaging</li><li>explain how the participants convey meaning through their use of linguistic and grammatical features.</li></ul>

English and English Language Teacher's Book Higher Tier
Section D: Spoken language

General resources

The resources in the Student Book, Teacher's Book and *kerboodle!* provide a range of learning opportunities for students and give them practice at developing their skills using a wide variety of text types. The resources suggested below can be used to reinforce, develop and extend students skills and learning further.

General resources	Author and title
Further reading	**Play scripts** *England People Very Nice* by Richard Bean – excellent play text that premiered at the National Theatre in 2009. Explores migration to the East End of London from the point of view of immigrants in a detention centre in the 21st century – the inmates are putting on a play about East End migration. By turns funny and sad, it explores how we are formed and how others judge us. It could be used as an interesting sideline through which to open up a debate about origins of language and culture. **Poetry** 'We Brits' by John Agard takes a satirical look at Britain from his perspective. Again, a good additional slant on the origins of language and its links to culture. **Reference materials and background reading** There are a number of books on language by David Crystal that could be used to provide an introduction to the topics covered in this unit, but in particular: *Txting: the gr8 db8*, David Crystal, OUP, 2008 *The Cambridge Encyclopaedia of the English Language,* David Crystal, CUP, 2003 Nelson Thornes' AS/A2 English Language Student Books for AQA contain sections on the development of spoken language and the influence of new technologies on language, which, again, could provide a useful introduction for teachers or offer extended reading for some students.
Websites	http://news.bbc.co.uk – the Magazine section of the BBC website often carries interesting and useful articles on the use of spoken language. www.askoxford.com – a resource based around the Oxford dictionaries, useful for 'new'/modern words added to the dictionary, with some fun and interesting resources. www.bl.uk – includes a good section on accent/dialect. Very interactive, complete with audio clips and regional input across the UK. www.bbc.co.uk/caribbean – the World Service's Caribbean page often has Caribbean patois-based articles and might be useful for engendering interest. www.skynewstranscripts.co.uk – useful resource, especially for sourcing scripts. The following websites make valuable links across the course and can be used to highlight the interrelated nature of the different areas of study: • www.benjaminzephaniah.com – fascinating performance website. He is very popular in all schools, but you might want to check this very thoroughly before offering a link! • www.poetryslam.org.uk – very popular with students.

29 Choosing and using language

AO focus

English Language AO2 Study of spoken language.

- Understand variations in spoken language, explaining why language changes in relation to contexts.
- Evaluate the impact of spoken language choices in their own and others' use.

In this chapter your students will:

- consider how purpose and audience affect how we speak
- examine how their speech is influenced by external factors
- develop skills in analysis of public speech.

Additional resources

Worksheets

29a: Purpose and audience

Getting started

It is unlikely that many students will have done much work on the study of spoken language prior to this chapter. This differs, then, from the other areas of study in the Student Book, where they are building on and developing skills they already have. They come to this 'fresh', with no preconceived notions of whether they are 'good' or 'bad' at it. It is important for them to realise at the outset that there are no right and wrong answers to many of the activities – simply findings. The activities are largely exploratory. In many cases the student is the expert. Indeed, when exploring their own idiolect, they are the only one who can do the task.

A simple starter would be to list pairs of words on the board and ask students to choose which ones they would use if talking to a small child. They could then explain their choices. Pairs of words could include:

- grimace/pull a face
- transform/change
- genuine/real
- consequence/result
- notorious/well-known.

You could then ask students to devise their own list of paired words and, if time permits, you could suggest they change the intended audience from a small child to, perhaps, another teenager. The aim of the task is to make clear that language use varies according to intended audience.

Working through the chapter

Purpose and audience

This section is intended to formalise what students already instinctively know about adapting speech to suit purpose and audience.

Activity 1 Appropriate choices would be:

- clear pronunciation
- eye contact
- appropriate clothing
- Standard English
- sit up straight
- smart appearance
- friendly manner
- punctuality
- smile
- knowledge about the shop.

Students are asked to place these in order of importance. You may wish to do this as a class activity and to discuss the priority students attribute to the different qualities and their reasons for this. The activity provides a useful opportunity to discuss the importance of personal presentation and how this can affect the outcome of an interview.

Activity 2 Two students role play two conversations based on the same situation and a third student feeds back his or her observations. As an alternative, you could do this as a class activity, with different students participating in the role plays and you collating feedback from the rest of the students. Reasons that might explain the differences include:

- informality/formality of situation
- how well Student B knows the person to whom they are speaking
- whether Student B wants to impress the friend
- respect for the adult figure of authority
- the responses given by Student C.

If appropriate to the students in the group, this activity offers an opportunity for discussion of inappropriate responses to figures of authority, such as police or teachers. Such responses can often lead to an undesirable escalation of a situation and students need to be made aware of this.

Activity 3 (Worksheet 29a) Students are asked to consider aspects of three recent conversations and identify differences between them and the reasons for these. Encourage them to think carefully about the actual words they used and to complete table similar to the one in the Student Book, in which they record a short extract showing part of what they said. They could work in pairs or small groups on this activity.

How speech is recorded

Audio case study activity: Transcripts

This section deals with how to record spoken language. Students will be familiar with the conventions of writing script, but are unlikely to have previous experience in this area. It would be helpful if students were given the opportunity, in groups of three, to read the transcript in the Student Book aloud, using the key to help them replicate the original conversation. Before moving on to Activity 4, you could ask them to continue the transcript for a few more lines.

Activity 4 Students are given the opportunity to practise what they have learned about writing a transcript, using examples from the previous activity as a starting point. As an alternative, you could ask them to work in pairs and to record a typical conversation that they would have with their partner.

Investigating your speech

Analysis activity: Dialect

Students have studied dialect and accent in Chapters 5 and 25, though you may wish to recap on their understanding of these terms. In this section they are going to explore other influences on the way they speak: their idiolect.

Activity 5

Webquest activity: Exploring dialect

Students first read the case study on Jacob (Text B), before identifying the influences on their idiolect. You may wish to present your personal case study for interest and to reinforce understanding, before asking students to complete this activity. You could cover all areas defined by points 1–7, and perhaps add one additional detail that has specific relevance for you. Once students have completed part (a), you may want to explore in more detail in class discussion the case studies of individual students with distinct characteristics. As always, when personal details are being revealed, it is best to seek the student's permission first, and better still to get them to do the explaining.

Activity 6

Learning activity: Jargon

Here students consider the language of social groups. This is an area in which the students are the experts and, generally, the teacher is the learner. You could start this activity by making clear that each group will be sharing its findings with the class and that you, as the learner, will be reporting back to the class the different things you have learned from them about the language of their social groups. Students often thrive when working with role reversal of this kind.

Activity 7 The correct groupings of the words is:

- **Football:** yellow card, wall, touchline, tackle, substitute, striker, shoot, red card, pitch, penalty, offside, league, hand ball, goalkeeper, foul, extra time, draw, dive, defender, corner kick, referee, goal, own goal.
- **Tennis:** ace, umpire, serve, set, tiebreaker, return, volley, rally, racquet, net, doubles, lob, line judge, groundstroke, let, match point, Grand Slam, forehand, backhand, advantage, deuce, break point, fault, crosscourt, double fault, Wimbledon.

Encourage students to compile their own lists of words relevant to a specific interest. As an extension of this activity, groups of students could randomly mix their lists of words and pass them on to another group to correctly match to specific areas.

Activity 8 In this activity students further explore influences on their own idiolect. The aim, again, is to raise their awareness of how and why they use language as they do. As before, you could extend your analysis of your own idiolect as a model for them. You could also ask them to create lists of words associated with the areas that have influenced them.

Before moving on to the section on Public speaking, you could ask students to write a detailed analysis of their idiolect, drawing on what they have learned from the chapter so far, with points being supported by extracts from transcripts of conversations.

Public speaking

Learning activity: Speeches

Having explored how students speak, the chapter moves on to explore the features of more formal

Chapter 29
Choosing and using language

public speaking. To do this, students consider an extract from a transcript of President Obama's inaugural speech. It is worth noting that transcripts of formal speeches are frequently recorded using the conventions of written English, as here. This is often because they start off as written texts, though intended for oral delivery.

There is a detailed commentary on the first four paragraphs of the speech. You could put each paragraph on the board and deal with the commentary for it, in turn. Alternatively, you could collate students' comments on each paragraph before turning to the commentaries in the Student Book.

Activities 9 and 10 Students now put into practice what they have learned from the analysis of the first four paragraphs.

If they have copies of Text E, they could highlight and annotate it. Remind them to look for the features listed in the activity, to comment on these and to share their ideas with other students. Some examples of what they might comment on are given below.

- **Third-person plurals:** 'we understand', 'who have carried us up', 'Our minds'.
- **Short sentences:** 'This is the journey we continue today', 'Our capacity remains undiminished'.
- **Ideas being developed:** the second and third paragraphs tell us more about the 'risk-takers, the doers, the makers of things'.
- **Shifts in tenses:** 'They saw America as ... This is the journey we ...'.
- **Reference to traditional values:** 'Our journey has never been one of shortcuts or settling for less'.
- **Groups of three:** 'It has not been the path for the fainthearted – for those who prefer leisure over work, or seek only the pleasures of riches and fame. Rather, it has been the risk-takers, the doers, the makers of things'.
- **Historical reference:** 'places like Concord and Gettysburg; Normandy and Khe Sahn'.
- **Emotive use of language:** 'they toiled in sweatshops', 'endured the lash of the whip and plowed the hard earth'.
- **Repetition:** 'Our workers ... Our minds ... Our capacity ...'.

Stretch yourself

These activities present students with the opportunity to extend their understanding of both idiolect and public speaking. For part **a**, it would be helpful for them to make a recording of a conversation with the elderly person, from which they could make a transcript. Remind students that they must always get a person's permission before recording what they say.

While part **b** suggests they comment on President Obama's delivery of his inaugural speech, from which the extracts are taken, they could, of course, watch any public speech and base their research on it.

Outcomes

In this chapter your students have:

- considered how purpose and audience affect how we speak
- examined the influences on their own idiolect
- considered the language of different groups
- developed their skills in analysis of public speech.

30 Multi-modal talk

AO focus

English Language AO2 Study of spoken language.

- Understand variations in spoken language, explaining why language changes in relation to contexts.
- Evaluate the impact of spoken language choices in their own and others' use.

In this chapter your students will:

- learn more about the features of spoken and written language
- identify the features of texting
- consider advantages and disadvantages of texting and instant messaging
- consider the relationship between instant messaging and spoken language.

Additional resources

Worksheets

30a: Differences between written and spoken language

30b: Full MSN chat

Getting started

As in the previous chapter, much of the work here is of an exploratory nature. There are often no right or wrong answers – simply findings. Many students are expert in both texting and 'conversing' online. Occasionally, sometimes for religious reasons, students choose not to text or engage in online chat. A useful starting point would be to collate students' own experiences of these areas. Questions such as the following would help to promote initial discussion:

- How many of you text?
- How regularly do you text?
- How many of you use internet chatrooms?
- How often and for how long do you use them?

In addition to the above, include students who do not use mobile phones or internet chatrooms by asking them to explain their reasons for not doing so. Depending on the students in your class, and their perspectives, you may want to spend some time on this discussion.

Working through the chapter

How we experience language

Activity 1 This is designed to prompt students to consider the ways in which they experience language and the areas of overlap between written and spoken language. For example, a Microsoft PowerPoint presentation is both heard and read. A public speech is both written and spoken.

Encourage students to make their initial list as comprehensive as possible. As an alternative approach, you could have students working in pairs or small groups from the beginning of the activity.

Once students have completed Activity 1, you might like to collate on the board areas that involve both spoken and written language.

Differences between written and spoken language

k! Learning activity: Language modes

k! Analysis activity: Urban bee-keeping

k! Learning activity: Features of spoken language

Having identified that there is overlap between written and spoken language, students now consider the key traditional features of each mode. This is likely to be an area that students have not previously considered, and you may want to check their understanding of keywords ('received', 'permanent', 'temporary', 'impersonal', 'personal', 'distant', 'immediate') before asking them to complete Activity 2.

Activity 2

An encyclopaedia entry ...	A telephone conversation ...
is received through the eyes.	is received through the ears.
is permanent in that it can be checked again and again.	is temporary in that it can only be retained in the memory.
is impersonal in that the audience is not known.	is personal in that it is directed to a specific audience.
is distant in that it can be accessed at any time.	is immediate in that it is restricted to the here and now.

It is made clear that the encyclopaedia entry and the telephone conversation are at the extremes of a continuum and that many types of language use have features of both written and spoken modes.

This division, however, is not always clear-cut, though there are some features that are more typical of one mode than the other.

Activity 3 (Worksheet 30a) The following is only one possible order of progressing from A to Z, though the letters attributed to each situation will vary from one student to another. There is no 'correct' answer.

Encyclopaedia entry; the Bible; telephone directory; political speech; church sermon; text message from a mobile phone company; a poem; play by Shakespeare; a shopping list; TV news broadcast; text message to a friend; reality TV programme; radio news broadcast; an internet chatroom; a class/group discussion; a phone call from a friend.

The important part of this activity is the thinking and discussion that accompanies it. You could collate the ideas and draw out further points for discussion. For example, you could consider whether the Bible, which is regularly read aloud in Christian churches, should be placed further along the continuum. An interesting point of discussion would be where to place 'a play by Shakespeare'. It was written with the sole intention of being heard, yet nowadays, many students' experience of a Shakespeare play is as a written text. Where might a 17th-century student have placed this?

Mixed modes

This section explores the features of texting and instant messaging. These are relatively new forms of communication, which clearly combine aspects of the written and spoken modes. As texting and messaging are changing and developing rapidly, it is possible that aspects of this section may become outdated quickly. Your students are likely to be up to date. Encourage students to identify any outdated areas and to inform you of the latest advances.

Texting

Activity 4

Analysis activity: Creative texting

a Students work together to identify possible reasons that would explain why texting has become so popular so quickly. These might include:
   - it is cheaper to text than phone
   - it started with young people so, initially, parents didn't really understand it
   - you can text without people knowing you're doing it
   - it makes people feel connected even when they are apart.

b Encourage every student to write a text. It would be helpful if these were written on A4 paper in a large font, but as they would appear on a mobile phone display.

c Students then work out and tabulate commonly used features of texting, based on their own examples.

d Encourage them to edit or add to the given list of features as appropriate. Remember that, as time progresses, this list of features is likely to become outdated.

e Students are directed to compare their table with another group's. You may prefer to collate the main features, with examples, on the board.

Activity 5 Help students to understand that the changes taking place in the use of language today are much greater than at any previous time in history. This is largely due to the speed with which changes and developments in both texting and messaging can be transmitted across the world. This activity seeks to reinforce their understanding of this by asking them to create a guide to texting for a student 50 years from now. Allow students to choose how they will structure and present their guide.

You could also encourage students to speculate about how electronic communication may develop over the next 50 years.

Activity 6

Viewpoints activity: Texting – good or bad?

The article 'Texting may be taking a toll' (Text B) is designed to promote consideration of the actual or potential disadvantages of texting. Many students have texted since they were young children and are unlikely to have seriously considered its negative features. This activity presents a useful opportunity for students to think about these in a structured way. It also provides the basis for a very interesting class discussion, should you wish to pursue this.

a The concerns expressed in the article include texting leading to:
   - anxiety
   - distraction
   - falling grades
   - repetitive strain injury
   - sleep deprivation
   - dependence of adolescents on their parents
   - young people not having clear time in which to think

- young people feeling frightened and overexposed
- temporary or permanent damage to thumbs.

b Possible additional points include:
- lack of privacy
- potential for bullying
- potential for cheating in exams.

c Clearly there is no correct order here. Encourage students to articulate their reasons for the order they select.

A useful extension to this activity would be to ask them to consider also the advantages of texting and to assess whether these outweigh the potential disadvantages. Alternatively, you could discuss whether mobile phones should or should not be allowed in schools, using your own school's policy on this as a starting point. In addition, you could extend the discussion to incorporate the dangers of internet chatrooms, the subject of the Stretch yourself activity at the end of this chapter.

Instant messaging

It is important that students understand the fundamental difference between texting and instant messaging in terms of communication. The parallel with leaving a message on an answerphone (texting) as opposed to having a conversation on the telephone might be useful here. As an alternative to using the transcript of an MSN conversation provided in the Student Book, you could ask students to provide their own transcripts of recent conversations they have taken part in online.

Activity 7 Here students are invited to note similarities and differences between the language used in texting and the language used in this MSN 'conversation' (Worksheet 30b provides an extended version). They could add details based on their own experiences of messaging.

Activity 8 This activity asks students to consider the features of instant messaging and the way in which it's like a conversation. It would be helpful for students to have a copy of the MSN text. They could then highlight, using different colours, the various threads of conversation. As in Activity 7, encourage students to use their own experiences of messaging to help them list reasons why turns are not always taken. They can also add their own examples of how writers help readers 'hear' how the words are said.

The rules

The final section of this chapter acts as a reminder that these forms of communication are in a state of flux and that the only way to keep in touch with the developments is to actually participate. You could ask students to consider how their transcripts of instant messaging differ from that provided in the Student Book, which was up to date at the time of going to press. This would illustrate the speed at which things change. It will also give students confidence in their expertise in this area.

> **Stretch yourself**
>
> Students have already considered the potential disadvantages of texting. This activity highlights some of the dangers of internet chatrooms and invites students to research this area further in preparation for writing a non-fiction article. As an alternative approach, you might want to use the given quotations as a starting point for group or class discussion. While it is good to draw students' attention to the potential dangers of internet chatrooms, it is also important to acknowledge the many positive experiences of people who visit them.

Outcomes

In this chapter your students have:

- learned about the main features of written and spoken language
- identified and written about the features of texting
- examined an extract of instant messaging
- considered different concerns about texting and messaging.

31 Making your spoken language study skills count in the controlled assessment

AO focus

English Language AO2 Study of spoken language.

- Understand variations in spoken language, explaining why language changes in relation to contexts.
- Evaluate the impact of spoken language choices in their own and others' use.

In this chapter your students will:

- learn about how the Spoken language study fits into their GCSE English Language course
- explore the Assessment Objectives for the Spoken language study
- look at the types of task they might undertake.

Additional resources

Worksheets
31a: Spoken genres

Working through the chapter

You could introduce this chapter by encouraging students to look at the world and 'listen' to it in a new way. As soon as you open a conversation about how we speak and how this affects what we say, they are immediately interested. If, at an early stage, this enthusiasm can be focused and directed to note-taking and observation, then the requirements of the controlled assessment will be much easier to achieve. This chapter is all about noting, exploring and explaining.

What is controlled assessment?

Controlled assessment is an opportunity for the students to show what they know in a set amount of time, without the pressure of having to go away and complete a great deal of work, drafting and redrafting their work and worrying about it over several weeks. It also means that the pressure of redraft marking on teaching staff is removed entirely and the focus is fully on learning and sharing information.

The controlled assessment is taken in conditions which are like an exam, but without the pressure. Brief notes will be allowed, but not drafts or essay outlines. For the Spoken language study students will be allowed to bring transcripts. They will also be allowed to use a dictionary or thesaurus to check their work.

You may choose to complete this work in a number of lessons to fit in with your timetable. If this is the case, the students will not be allowed to take any work away with them; it will be kept securely until the next session. You may choose to allow computer access to complete the work. In this case, the students are not allowed general access to the internet (only to source work such as transcripts or video clips that have been stored previously) and their work will be stored on a secure server so that it cannot be accessed when they have left the room and feel the urge to carry on working!

Your guidance of students in this work is extremely important. You may choose to source a transcript for your entire group to use (being aware of copyright restrictions) or they may produce their own transcripts. It is advisable to stress to the students the need for a good quantity of material in order to effect a good basis for analysis. This is something that most students find very difficult and time-consuming, and it can detract from the assessment task itself. It could be wise, therefore, to teach the differing areas of study and gauge the interest of the group. Then you will be in a better position to target the selection of transcript material to support their controlled assessment task. It would still be a good idea to provide variety, as this gives an element of personal learning and acknowledges that we do not all think in the same way. This is something the students will really appreciate and it will bring good dividends with not much extra input. There are a number of transcript resources available legally online which can provide a good basis for analysis.

If students do source their own material, please warn them about copyright restrictions and remind them that they cannot record conversations without permission!

Introducing the tasks

This section of the Student Book explains the three headings under which the Spoken language study tasks will fall:

- Social attitudes to spoken language
- Spoken genres
- Multi-modal talk.

English and English Language Teacher's Book Higher Tier
Section D: Spoken language

The Assessment Objectives are given and explained in more student-friendly language. It is worth spending time so that Students understand these.

When students are preparing material they should remember what the AOs are asking of them. They will need to:

- show that they know why people speak in different ways at different times and in different places
- make comments (good and bad) about the effects of the language that people choose to use.

Once the students have gathered their information, they need to think about the most important points that their data gives them. They will need to note different things, for example:

- word use – how and why different words are used
- frequency of words
- jargonised words
- word deviations in text or MSN speak.

Sample tasks and sample answers

This section of the chapter provides a simple, uncluttered outline suggestion for an essay structure with which students could approach any of the tasks. This means that it can be adapted for the students' needs, but actually gives them all they need to structure a good analytical essay. It enables the students to explore for themselves and develop an individual approach to planning and writing, which is ideal for the higher-tier candidate.

In the written assignment students will need to be able to explain and evaluate what they have been studying. They will need to show their understanding of the topic. Their key skills will need to be exploration and analysis. This means that for the top marks they will need to do more than simply describe what they did and what they were looking at. As they explore students will give evidence (quotations) and support these with developed comment about what they show and what they have found. The more selective they are about this, the better – simply quoting chunks of text cannot deliver the best essays.

Social attitudes to spoken language

On your marks activity: The Spoken language study controlled assessment 1

This topic area deals with how we perceive language and how we react to it. It is an interesting area of study that will involve the exploration of how different people talk and how this language use changes with generations and situations.

The key words for this topic will be 'reflect' or 'investigate'. A sample task is given in the Student Book.

Activity 1

a   Students are asked to consider a response to the given task. You may find it is more productive for them to work in pairs or small groups on this task, and a photocopy of the student response for highlighting of the different specified areas would also be helpful.

b   Below are examples of what students might identify to match the bullet points. Aim to discuss their choices and the reasons for them.

- **A brief outline of the background:** contained in the introduction.
- **Selection of detail to illustrate the points:** 'He mentioned money a few times when he spoke. He talked about "savings"'. References to 'saving the coppers' and 'Post Office savings book'.
- **Identification of the origin of words:** explanation that 'beehive' was a fiver – Cockney rhyming slang for 'five'.
- **Exploration of why words are used in certain situations:** suggestion that reference to 'bees' must have something to do with working hard.
- **Reflection on the use of language:** 'Many of the words were very colourful and showed very clearly how much people were focused on saving when he was a boy'.

c   Students are asked to read the teacher's comments and work out what the student needs to do in order to improve. Encourage them to express these in their own words and remind them that these are skills they should be aiming to demonstrate in their assignments. They should identify:

- the need to explore futher
- examine the origins of words in more detail
- consider how language has changed over time
- analyse language use more closely by focusing on the context in which specific words or phrases occurred.

Spoken genres

On your marks: The Spoken language study controlled assessment 2

There are elements of this topic area which are similar to that of Social attitudes to spoken language, particularly in the way that students are asked to explore how language works in different situations and for different reasons.

The key words for this topic will be 'how' something is 'represented' or 'investigate'.

Activity 2 (Worksheet 31a) This activity encourages the students to really think about the connotations of the language we use and the effects this has. They need to be aware of the power of language in order to fully analyse the spoken form. This is a task that can be adapted to be used as a quick 10-minute starter activity, enabling students to develop a reflex response to language analysis and moving towards a point where they will be able to demonstrate a depth of analysis with ease.

- What are the connotations of these words?
- What other words would they link to?
- Are they words that float somewhere in the middle of meaning or are their meanings very black and white?

For example:

- **Hero:** This is a word that only carries positive connotations. A hero is someone to look up to, in whatever situation they find themselves. It is a powerful word that 'feels' alive , 'feels' strong and forceful. Yet the person does not need to be powerful, they can be relatively weak, but looked up to anyway because of their actions. It is an all-powerful word, one which is forthright and unambiguous.

- **Cult figure:** This is someone who is almost worshipped by sectors of society. It does not carry the same unambiguous nature as 'hero', and can be applied to figures who might not be completely pure and wholesome. The word 'cult' suggests a blind following, regardless of reason. It suggests that there is something almost mesmeric about the person which throws reason out of the window and compels you to follow.

Multi-modal talk

Planning activity: The Spoken language study controlled assessment 3

This is a topic area that many students will be particularly interested in. It allows them to explore and explain things like instant messaging and text speak. It is an area that is fast-moving and literally evolving as it is used.

The key words for this topic will be 'how', relating to the practicalities of the actual communication;

'what devices' is linked to this and they will be asked to link their discoveries to real speech. They are being asked to explore the links between this written communication and how it can be considered a relation of spoken language.

Activity 3 This activity builds on the structuring skills that have been highlighted in the previous tasks, and encourages students to begin to use their developing analytical skills to write a short paragraph. This will help them to become more relaxed about the requirements of this unit, as well as developing their ability to write well in a limited timescale.

It might be easier to break this question down a little and consider the following with your students:

- What are the differences between texting/messaging and normal written communication?
- How do these differences make texting/messaging closer to spoken than written language?

For example, normal written communication is often much more formalised than texting/messaging, and relies on the use of punctuation for meaning. It can be extremely important that written communication is clear and unambiguous. This is important, whether the purpose of the task is a letter of application, a letter of complaint or a love letter! It is very important to convey the message in a precise and clear manner.

In contrast, texting and messaging are shorthand, speedy forms of communication which do not need to be as accurate as the more traditional written form. In this way they are much closer to spoken language, as they are spontaneous and immediate. They are relatively unconsidered and not nearly as precise as the true written form. This is something we do not think about in everyday speech because we are so used to it. We are normally quite good at just speaking and 'editing' and adjusting our speech as we go along. This brings texting and messaging very close to spoken language and moves them further from written speech.

Outcomes

In this chapter your students have:

- learned about how spoken language fits into their GCSE English language course
- learned more about the ways they can achieve high marks in this part of the course.

English essentials

Punctuation

Capital letters

Activity 1 The following punctuation reflects a likely choice, although students could have placed exclamation marks at the end of the 2nd or 4th sentences.

> Have you ever read a book you just couldn't put down? Well, if not, you need to try *Smokescreen*. It's the action book with everything needed to keep you on the edge of your seat until the very last page. Like all the other books in this series, this one's a winner. Read it now!

Commas

Activity 2 The following punctuation reflects correct usage.

> Your computer can catch a virus from disks, a local network or the internet. Just as a cold virus attaches itself to a human host, a computer virus attaches itself to a program and, just like a cold, it is contagious. Like viruses, worms replicate themselves. However, instead of spreading from file to file, they spread from computer to computer, infecting an entire system.

Colons/semicolons

Activity 3 Students could check each other's examples for correct usage of colons and semicolons.

Apostrophes

Activity 4 Apostrophes should have been used as follows.

> I'd really like to join you on your birthday. Unfortunately, I've a meeting planned for the same date. I'll try to leave early so I shouldn't be too late. It'll be good to see you again. Hope you're keeping well and haven't had too many problems with work.

Activity 5 Apostrophes should have been used as follows.

> John's mother told him not to go to Peter's house during the week's holiday. However, he borrowed his brother's bike and went straight there. There was no one in, though the younger children's toys were out on the lawn. Peter's window was open and John climbed through it to wait for him. Unfortunately, he was spotted by the neighbour's dog and then by the neighbour.

Inverted commas

Activity 6 Students match the rules to various parts of the extract.

- **The spoken words are contained within inverted commas**
  For example: 'I'm sorry'
- **Each new piece of speech starts with a capital letter**
  For example: 'There really shouldn't be a problem'
- **Each piece of speech ends with a punctuation mark**
  For example: '... I can't let you in.'
- **A new line is started each time there is a new speaker**
  For example: 'Rules are rules'

Activity 7 Students are requested to study the extract and the annotations. You may wish to do this on the whiteboard as a class activity.

Activity 8 Inverted commas and a colon should have been added as follows.

> It is as though Larkin believes that 'being beautiful' can be 'unworkable'. In contrast, being 'not ugly, not good-looking' can bring greater happiness, perhaps because you put more effort into being happy. It is for this reason that he wishes she should:
>
> 'Have, like other women,
>
> An average of talents.'

Spelling

Syllables

Activity 9 The aim of this activity is to help students to break words down. Students may have put breaks in slightly different places, though likely choices are:

1 2 3 4 5 ex/tra/ord/in/ary	1 2 3 4 par/li/a/ment	1 2 3 4 en/vi/ron/ment
1 2 3 4 re/min/is/cent	1 2 3 4 5 con/sci/en/tious/ly	1 2 3 4 5 ne/cess/a/ril/y

Suffixes

Activity 10 Students will compile lists of varied lengths. An example is:

> wondered   wondering   wonderingly

Encourage students to swap answers to see which pair can come up with the most words.

Prefixes

Activity 11 The aim is to get students thinking about the use of prefixes. Once the activity is completed, you could get them to check their 'new' words in a dictionary.

Combining suffixes and prefixes

Activity 12 Again, students are encouraged to 'create' words using prefixes and suffixes. One example is:

> disagree
>
> disagreeable
>
> disagreeably
>
> disagreement
>
> disagreeing
>
> disagreed

Plurals

Activity 13 Plurals are as follows.

branches	holidays	Christmases	beaches	radii or radiuses
ladies	atlases	inches	women	blushes
comedies	cacti or cactuses	takeaways	hoaxes	witches
berries	bonuses	pluses	essays	gases
arches				

Homonyms

Activity 14 Homonyms are as follows.

sea/see	pour/pore	great/grate	rowed/road	way/weigh
piece/peace	profit/prophet	soul/sole	lone/loan	pair/pear
hole/whole	hare/hair	hymn/him	ate/eight	

Activity 15 There are many possibilities. Here are just a few:

allowed/aloud	ceiling/sealing	new/knew
raise/rays	teas/tease	you/ewe

How a dictionary is organised

Students cannot use a dictionary effectively without a firm grasp of alphabetical order. This section focuses on developing that skill.

Activity 16 The correct order for each group of words is as follows:

- best, drastic, envelope, free, icing, money, public, risk, silver, trial
- range, rattle, ready, reason, red, rider, ring, robot, roller, rush
- grid, grief, grievance, grill, grime, grin, grind, grip, grit, grizzly

Activity 17 Students should have come up with the following solution for finding these words in the dictionary:

- 'skull' – page 968
- 'skate' – page 966
- 'skyscraper' – page 969
- 'skill' – page 967.

Activity 18 Students struggle to find words in the dictionary when they do not know the correct spelling. For this activity, ask them to focus on what they do know and what they can work out about the word to help them locate it in the dictionary.